THE BEST OF
Birds&Blooms

Ruby-throated hummingbird, page 112

Table *of* Contents

ON THE FRONT COVER
Baltimore oriole in cherry blossoms. Photo by Bill Leaman

ON THE BACK COVER
Black swallowtail butterfly on gooseneck loosestrife. Photo by Amy Tipton, Erwin, Tennessee

*Red admiral
butterfly, page 214*

Introduction

Take a look at the latest in the world of birding and gardening with this brand-new edition of *The Best of Birds & Blooms.*

Learn exciting facts, such as how birds use their senses; read about popular species, like orioles and sandhill cranes; get the scoop on attracting more desirable birds to your backyard; and find out what is essential to have for an ideal habitat. You can attract hummingbirds and keep them coming back for more!

Discover gardening tips from the pros that will help you beautify your landscape. Create the backyard oasis of your dreams for butterflies and beneficial bugs. Plus, enjoy a whole section full of practical expert advice on birds and plants, including identification and bird feeder know-how.

This book is jam-packed with birding pointers, gardening how-to's, stunning photos submitted by readers from coast to coast—and more. We hope you learn from the bonus resource section, too!

—*The editors of* Birds & Blooms *magazine*

Baltimore oriole,
page 135

Editorial

ASSOCIATE CREATIVE DIRECTOR:
Christina Spalatin

DEPUTY EDITOR:
Kirsten Sweet

ART DIRECTOR:
Sharon Nelson

ASSOCIATE EDITOR:
Julie Kuczynski

LAYOUT DESIGNER:
Carole Ross

COPY EDITOR:
Chris McLaughlin

PRODUCTION ARTIST:
Jill Banks

SENIOR RIGHTS ASSOCIATE:
Jill Godsey

Contributors

Lisa Ballard, Kenn and Kimberly Kaufman, Ken Keffer, Heather Lamb, Rachael Liska, Luke Miller, Melinda Myers, Rob Ripma, Kelsey Roseth, Sally Roth, David W. Shaw, Jill Staake, Tom Watson, Deb Wiley

© 2019 RDA Enthusiast Brands, LLC.
1610 N. 2nd St., Suite 102, Milwaukee, WI 53212-3906

International Standard Book Number:
978-1-61765-848-8

International Standard Serial Number: 1553-8400

Component Number:
118500051H

CHAPTER 1

The JOYS of Bird-watching

From colorful feathers to the cadence of their songs, there's so much to love about birds!

Eight Shades of *Orange*

Eye-catching orioles come decked out in warm hues and build unique, pouch-shaped nests that hang from branches. Get to know each member of this colorful clan.

A FLASH OF GLOWING ORANGE among the pale green new leaves and a melodious whistle floating on the breeze—after you've seen an oriole on a spring morning, you'll understand why these songbirds are perennial favorites. The Baltimore oriole, common all over the East in the warmer months, is the most famous member of the clan, but you can see seven additional species across North America.

"Oriole" is based on several Latin words that all mean "golden." The name was first applied to a European bird, a member of what is now called the Old World oriole family. However, American orioles are completely unrelated and classified in the blackbird family, along with other birds such as grackles, red-winged blackbirds and meadowlarks. The tropics of Mexico and Central and South America are home to more than 30 species of orioles, so the eight found north

A Baltimore oriole on a crabapple tree is a common spring sight in the East.

of the Texas-Mexico border are just the tip of the colorful iceberg.

In most familiar oriole species, females mainly wear hues of greenish yellow to orange-yellow and are not as brightly colored as males. Females do most of the work of building the nests and incubating the eggs, but males do chip in to help feed the young.

The female orioles deserve lots of credit as remarkable builders. Their nests are marvels of avian architecture: hanging pouches or bags of tightly woven plant fibers, attached by their edges and suspended from twigs. Many oriole nests are deeper than they are wide, and despite their distinctive appearance, they can be hard to spot, because they're often surrounded by heavy foliage. Backyard birders often discover they have an oriole nest in their trees only after the leaves have fallen in autumn.

Here's where and how to spot every oriole species regularly found in the U.S. and Canada.

THE BACKYARD SUPERSTARS:
Baltimore, Bullock's and Orchard
Decked out in orange and black, male Baltimore and Bullock's orioles add dazzling color to backyards in summer—Baltimores in the East, Bullock's in the West. Where they meet on the western Great Plains, the two sometimes interbreed, creating hybrids. For a few years they were categorized into one species called

Orchard oriole

Bullock's oriole

"Northern oriole," and you can still find that name in some older books. Most fly to the tropics for the winter, but increasing numbers of Baltimore orioles are now staying through the cold months in some eastern states where people keep feeders filled to attract them.

Widespread in the East and parts of the Southwest in summer, orchard orioles are smaller than other orioles, and adult males have a unique color combination with deep chestnut instead of orange and yellow.

THE SOUTHWEST DUO:
Hooded and Scott's
In summer, hooded orioles are common from coastal California to southern Texas, chiefly in lowland riversides, canyons and backyards. They often place their nests in palm trees, using the long, strong fibers of palm leaves as nesting material. But if no palms are available, they'll readily nest in sycamores, cottonwoods or other trees. Adult males are primarily orange (including an orange "hood") with black accents.

Scott's orioles are found ranging from eastern California and northern Utah to the central Texas Hill Country. Open woodlands of juniper or oak may be good habitats for them, but they're especially drawn to areas with lots of yucca plants, building their nests among the long, daggerlike yucca leaves. The rich, bubbling song of the male Scott's oriole carries for long distances across arid hillsides.

THE TROPICAL TRIO:
Altamira, Audubon's and Spot-breasted
The southern tip of Texas is home to two of the lesser known orioles, Altamira and Audubon's. Unlike the more northern species, these two are nonmigratory, sticking around all winter in that subtropical climate. Another difference from their northern cousins: the sexes look the same. Both male and female Altamira orioles look like supersized male hooded orioles. The female

Scott's oriole on blooming ocotillo

Altamira builds an astounding nest, a hanging bag of plant fibers that may be 2 feet long, sometimes suspended from telephone wires.

Audubon's orioles are not so flamboyant; both males and females are mainly yellow, with black head, wings and tail. The Audubon's song is slow and hesitant, like a person learning how to whistle.

In the past, southern Florida had no orioles in the summer, just Baltimore and orchard orioles during migration and winter. But some spot-breasted orioles—native to Central America and sometimes kept as cage birds—escaped from captivity near Miami in the 1940s and established a population in suburbs around southeastern Florida. This is another tropical species in which the males and females look alike.

With all these possibilities, you have a chance to see one or more kinds of orioles practically anywhere. And with a little luck, these golden birds may treat you to a glimpse right outside your own window.

An Audubon's (left) and Altamira oriole share a stump.

It's impossible to tell whether this is a male or female spot-breasted oriole: They are identical!

HOW TO ATTRACT ORIOLES

Bring these colorful songsters to your yard with these expert tips.

NATIVE TREES
Orioles love trees, especially native varieties. The top choices will depend on where you live, but elms, cottonwoods and sycamores are typically good options.

FLOWERS
More than most songbirds, orioles love nectar, and they may visit some of the same tubular red flowers that attract hummingbirds.

SUGAR WATER
Orioles will come to feeders that contain a mix of one part sugar to four parts water. No artificial coloring needed! Regular hummingbird feeders work if they have perches, or you can buy orange-colored feeders designed for orioles.

ORANGES
Half of a fresh orange, impaled on a stick, makes an easy and irresistible snack for orioles.

OTHER FOODS
A small dish of grape jelly may attract orioles, catbirds and other popular backyard fliers. Live or dried mealworms might draw a crowd as well.

Name that *Tune*

Take on the challenge of identifying birds by their sweet melodies. It's easy with these expert tips.

STEP INTO THE BACKYARD on a summer morning and you're likely to be greeted by a chorus of chirps and trills. Robins are caroling and chickadees are singing *chickadee-dee-dee-dee*. Suddenly, a different tune, a snappy *wichity-wichity*, stands out from the others. A search along the hedge just behind the garden reveals a yellowthroat, a new bird for your yard!

Almost all birds make some kind of sounds, and most give both calls and songs. Calls are usually short notes, like the *tchip* from a cardinal, and you may hear them in all seasons. Songs are usually longer and more complicated, and they're typically heard in spring and summer. Any time is a good time to begin birding by ear.

Start with Your Backyard Friends

Because learning all of the songs may seem overwhelming at first, remember that you don't have to master every one at once. A good way to narrow it down is to begin at home, focusing on the songs of your most common backyard visitors. Spring and summer are when birds are most vocal, so make plans to spend extra time outdoors in those seasons. Watch the chickadees, nuthatches, goldfinches and jays in your yard, but listen to them, too. After learning to recognize backyard feathered friends by voice, build on that baseline knowledge to identify other birds in your area.

A house wren sings a fast, musical verse from the stem of a smooth oxeye sunflower.

Branch Out

A visit to wildlife hot spots provides an opportunity to search for birds in different habitats. Investing the time to learn which birds prefer wetlands, forest or grasslands will help to narrow down the number of bird species you consider. For example, chipping sparrows and swamp sparrows sing similar songs but prefer different habitats. If you are near a big marsh and hear a bird singing a rapid series of chip notes, chances are good that it's a swamp sparrow. A similar song in your backyard, with no wetland habitat nearby, is more likely to be from a chipping sparrow.

Tricks of the Trade

When you listen to a bird's song, take an extra step and describe it to yourself. Is it a long song or a short one? Is the tone clear, buzzy or rough? Is the pitch high or low? Are some sounds repeated over and over? Thinking about these questions, and even writing down a description of the song, will help to cement it firmly in your memory.

Speaking of memory, a mnemonic (the first "m" is silent) is a learning trick that helps you remember things. If you can match the pattern of a birdsong to a series of words, that mnemonic will help you remember it later. For instance, it might be easier to recall the eastern towhee's three-part song if you think of it as saying *drink your tea.* Or the yellow warbler's lovely song as *sweet-sweet-sweet, I am so sweet.* And while some birders hear the white-throated sparrow singing *oh, sweet Canada-Canada-Canada,* others think it sounds more like *old Sam Peabody-Peabody-Peabody.*

Practicing birdsong mnemonics can also be a fun game to play with kids. Youngsters get a kick out of repeating the song of a Carolina wren as *teakettle-teakettle-teakettle.* Or the tune the American goldfinch sings during its bouncy flight as *potato chip, potato chip, potato chip.* Or the magnificent barred owl's hooting as *who cooks for you? who cooks for you all?*

Tools of the Trade

From books and CDs to YouTube tutorials and many phone apps, birders will find a plethora of tools for learning bird songs. And while many of these tools are very helpful, there's no replacement for spending time outside watching for birds and listening as they sing.

One important point to remember about using birdsong apps for your phone: Use them carefully while in the field because birds are sensitive to disturbances, especially during nesting season. When a nesting bird hears a song from an app, it my leave the nest to defend its territory from the "intruder." This can cause the nest to fail. At some wildlife areas and parks, playing bird songs is actually illegal. Your highest priority should be respecting the birds in their environment.

Birding by ear also boosts the number of birds you find and identify and adds to the enjoyment of your time outdoors. With some patience and practice, you'll appreciate the voices of birds as much as their colorful plumage.

A yellow warbler may repeat its sweet song up to 10 times per minute.

KNOW WHAT YOU HEAR

Separate sounds into categories to help you distinguish songs from one another.

Caroling: rich, varied and musical, like a robin.

Trill: fast, flat series of notes, like a chipping sparrow.

High-pitched: high, thin notes, like a cedar waxwing or brown creeper.

Whistles: clear notes, like a northern cardinal.

Chirp: short and simple, like the notes of a house sparrow.

Scream: clear or harsh, like the cry of a red-tailed hawk.

A pair of adult sandhill cranes

Get to Know Sandhills

Meet the prehistoric bird that has been around for 2 million years.

200

During migration, these cranes may travel more than 200 miles a day. They're fast fliers, reaching speeds of up to 35 miles per hour.

75

During migration, 75 percent of the population can be found along a 75-mile stretch of the Platte River in Nebraska.

2.5

The oldest known sandhill crane fossil was found in the Macasphalt Shell Pit in Florida and is estimated to be 2.5 million years old.

32

A female sandhill crane usually lays two pale-colored eggs with brown markings. She shares incubation duties with her mate for up to 32 days.

8

Sandhill crane offspring can be ready to leave the nest and even start swimming just eight hours after they hatch. Although the chicks are independently mobile, they will stay with their parents up to 10 months after being born.

90

Most of their diet (90 percent) is plant material, including waste grain, roots, berries and nuts. Insects and snails are on the menu, too.

Birding *Beyond* the Backyard

Grab a pair of binoculars and a field guide, then set out to see more species than you ever have before.

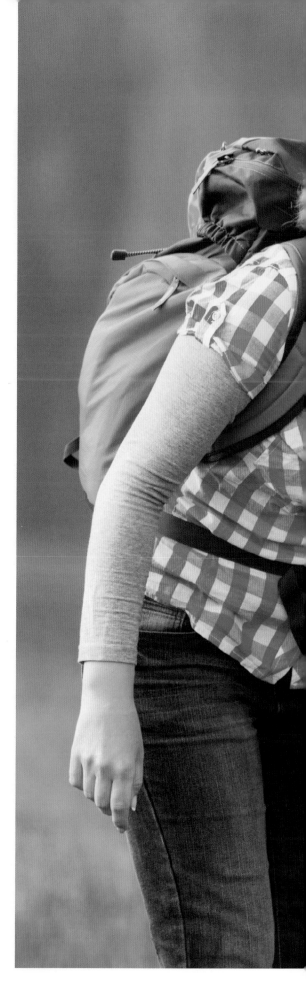

WATCHING A BUSY BACKYARD FEEDER from your living room window is always fun and exciting, but there's a wider world of birds waiting to be explored. Species as diverse as tiny yellow warblers and majestic bald eagles don't usually stop by feeders. To see these birds and other far-flung fliers, you have to go to them, especially during spring migration.

For many beginning and intermediate birders, knowing where and how to start bird-watching outside of their backyards is a challenge. To get started, try these three simple steps.

Get the Right Tools

When it comes to becoming a bona fide birder, all you need is a pair of binoculars and a good field guide.

Binoculars are the single most important tool for a birder. A good pair gets you a sharp view of each bird so you can figure out what species you're seeing. But selecting the right binoculars can be tricky, because prices and quality vary.

DO IT TOGETHER
Grab the binoculars and set out on a birding scavenger hunt with your favorite kid. Create a list of common birds for them to spot, like cardinals, blue jays, robins and chickadees.

To see birds like magnolia warblers, leave your backyard behind and head to the woods.

DO IT TOGETHER

Keep a notebook together of your bird observations. Kids will learn to notice field marks, behaviors and habitats. It's a great way to look back on your family's outdoor adventures!

For beginning birders, go with a pair priced between $150 and $300 and labeled 8x42; 8 is the magnification and 42, the lens size. The higher the numbers, the more you will be able to see, but these models are pricier and heavier.

The Vortex Diamondback 8x42 and Celestron Nature DX 8x42 are two solid choices that will not break the bank but will put a reliable set of bins in your hands.

Celestron's Nature DX 8x42 bins are low-cost and reliable.

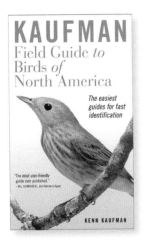

A quality field guide will help you narrow down and identify species you don't recognize. It also covers the distinguishing marks you'll need to get to know so you can tell the difference between males and females of the same species, or between adults and juveniles.

Of the very many excellent field guides out there, two great choices are *Kaufman Field Guide to Birds of North America* by Kenn Kaufman, and *The Sibley Guide to Birds* by David Allen Sibley. The latter also comes in two region-specific editions, one for the West and one for the East.

Choose Your First Birding Stop

With your binoculars and field guide in hand, it's time to pick where you want to go birding. The best place to begin is a local park, which gives you a chance to see and learn about a few new-to-you species while spotting some that are familiar visitors at your backyard feeder. This is also a wonderful way to meet and make friends with other enthusiasts.

When you're ready to explore beyond nearby green spaces, use eBird's Hotspot Explorer (*ebird.org/ebird/hotspots*) to find other good birding spots in your area. Put in the name of a place to learn what birds have been spotted there, and then get a checklist you can use while you're out in the field.

Once you find a site you'd like to visit, consider checking in with a local Audubon Society chapter for specific directions and tips for birding in the area. Over 450 chapters around the country provide a wealth of local information, such as best places to go birding and how to get reports of rare species that have been spotted. Many provide beginning birder walks and educational programming. Go to *audubon.org/about/audubon-near-you* to find the one closest to you or to an area you want to explore.

As you continue to expand your horizons, you may want to travel farther to see region-specific species, like California scrub-jays, found only along the West Coast, or great crested flycatchers in the East. Whether you decide to drive a couple states over or fly to a different country, there are endless opportunities to look for amazing birds and get to know other birders.

If you really want to experience the birding community, attend a bird festival. Regardless of how skilled you are at birding, some of the best include the Biggest Week in American Birding in Ohio (*biggestweekinamericanbirding.com*), the Rio Grande Valley Birding Festival in southern Texas (*rgvbf.org*) and the Space Coast Birding Festival in Florida (*spacecoastbirding.com*).

These events focus on specific bird-watching opportunities, like the warbler migration at the Biggest Week, but they also often host programs that are entertaining and informative, as well as seminars and panels led by experts.

Keep Learning

People who've been birding for a long time will tell you they never stop learning. You'll almost always discover something new about these wonderful fliers.

The Internet is a seemingly infinite resource for birders, and if you haven't already connected with the National Audubon Society (*audubon.org*), it's a valuable source of information. Other fantastic national organizations with thorough websites (everything from bird news to species profiles and ranges) include the Cornell Lab of Ornithology (*allaboutbirds.org*), the American Birding Association (*aba.org*) and Bird Studies Canada (*birdscanada.org*). The organizations also focus on conservation, an important consideration for anyone who enjoys being outside.

Then there's social media. Facebook pages focusing on birds are booming, from small local groups to state pages that post national rare bird alerts. Search around a little to see what you can find that matches your specific interests.

Birding is about more than just seeing new species. It's about the people, too. When you step out of your backyard, you step into a community that cares deeply about nature and sharing its passion for birds. Welcome to the club!

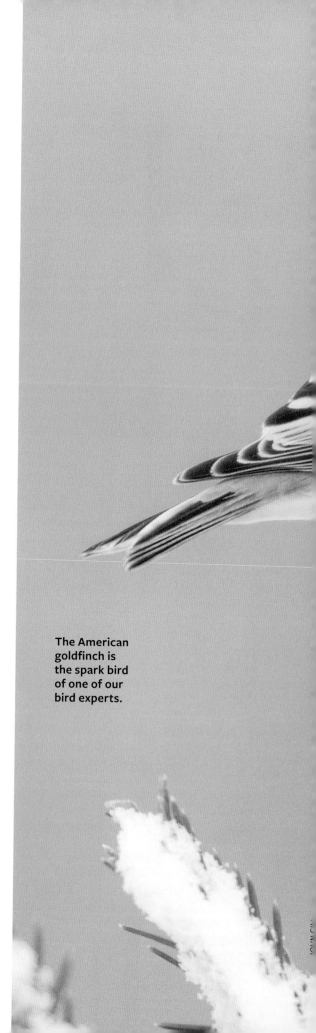

Spark Birds

From robins to wrens, all it takes is one species and a special moment to ignite a lifelong passion.

WHAT'S YOUR SPARK BIRD? Ask that question to a group of birders and get ready for a wide range of answers and heartwarming stories. A "spark bird" is lingo for the species that first ignited someone's interest in birding. Whether that moment leads to an entire career dedicated to ornithology or a lifelong bird-watching hobby, it's hard to forget the bird that started it all.

American Goldfinch

I grew up in the country and spent nearly every waking moment of my childhood playing outside. But it was a revelation when, in my late 20s, I discovered the world of birds. I was at an appointment in a small town not far from our family farm when I noticed movement outside the window. There was a bird feeder, and every

perch was occupied by dazzling male American goldfinches. When I asked, in stunned amazement, what they were, the response was, "Um, they're just goldfinches. They're very common birds in this area."

The entire course of my life changed in that single moment. I was determined to help other people discover birds and the natural world. Eventually, I got involved with Black Swamp Bird Observatory, where I helped start the Ohio Young Birders Club and the Biggest Week in American Birding. Birds gave me a purpose, and I can never do enough to repay all the joy they've brought to my life.

Kimberly Kaufman *Oak Harbor, Ohio*

The American goldfinch is the spark bird of one of our bird experts.

A peregrine falcon sighting influenced one woman's career choice.

Peregrine Falcon

After I graduated from college, I knew I wanted to pursue a career in wildlife conservation and decided to volunteer at a local nature center so I could teach visitors about the amazing hawks, owls and other birds of prey that live around us.

A few days later, as I was telling my mom about my plans over cups of coffee, I saw a

peregrine falcon land in a tree just outside the living room window. Because it was large and female peregrine falcons tend to be bigger than males, I believe it was female. She was perched on a bare branch about two feet away from the window, giving us the perfect view. She stayed for several minutes, preening and showing off her pointed wings and barred chest pattern. At one point, she even looked at me!

I'd never seen a peregrine falcon up close in the wild before, and certainly not in my front yard. This once-endangered species had been a rare sight for decades, but conservation efforts have helped their populations to slowly recover. Seeing that falcon was a truly special moment. Not only did it further cement my drive to work in conservation, but it also sparked my interest in birds that inhabit or migrate through urban areas. (Did you know that peregrine falcons sometimes nest in skyscrapers?)

Years after that front-yard encounter, I'm now employed by the same nature center where I first volunteered. Every day I get to share my peregrine falcon experience with new birders and hear what their spark birds are.

Michelle Allison *Milwaukee, Wisconsin*

House Sparrow

As silly as it sounds, my spark bird is the house sparrow. I saw those tiny birds everywhere as they gobbled up food crumbs that had fallen on the pavement. I wanted to know what they were, so I went out and bought my first field guide. From there, I never looked back.

Megan Blackwell *Conneaut, Ohio*

Pileated Woodpecker

A pileated woodpecker had been haunting a nearby woodland when I was 10 years old, so one day my father, who was a wildlife photographer, took me on a search for the bird. At the time, the species was extremely rare in southwestern Ohio. We tracked down the woodpecker—and what a truly amazing sight (and sound) it was!

Within a decade, my father, Karl, and I started pursuing pileateds with cameras in hand. The birds always look so majestic in pictures. After I graduated from Brown University, I went to work full-time with my father. My brother, Dave, joined the business, too. Today, I'm still grateful for that first pileated woodpecker. It ignited a fire that grew as I learned more about the interconnectedness of birds and nature.

Steve Maslowski *Cincinnati, Ohio*

Yellow-Shafted Northern Flicker

It was spring, and we had just moved to a new house. One morning, with the windows open, we heard a bird making a quick *wick-a* call. I thought someone's pet parrot had escaped! When I kept hearing that same sound day after day, I was intrigued, so I downloaded a bird app to solve the mystery. I found a woodpecker call that sounded similar but wasn't quite right. I went through bird after bird, not realizing that not every woodpecker has "woodpecker" in its name. Finally...eureka! It was a northern flicker!

The next morning, I got up early and sat near the bedroom window to wait. The flicker flew in and started drumming on a nearby electrical pole. It was the most glorious sight I had ever seen, from its black bib to its nifty polka dots. I never knew such a bird existed.

Later on, my wife connected me with a friend who is a birder. He took me birding, and I've been hooked ever since. I still appreciate that northern flicker for the awakening.

Bobby Hiebert Jr. *Salina, Kansas*

The eye-catching red crest of a pileated woodpecker inspired a wildlife photographer.

Northern Cardinal

The bird that first sparked my interest in birding and the outdoors is the northern cardinal. As a young child I was very fond of the color red, and my mom would often take my siblings and me to the Toledo Metroparks, where my love for flashy red cardinals bloomed.

After countless visits to our local library for field guides (and returning many overdue books), I soon realized there was a lot more to birding than just my spark bird, and my interest in cardinals expanded to other birds in Ohio, then to all North American birds.

When I was a beginner on birding trips, I wouldn't even count the other birds until I saw at least one northern cardinal. Today, I lead trips for the Toledo Naturalists' Association, the Ohio Young Birders Club and the Black Swamp Bird Observatory, among others.

I owe so much to the brilliantly beautiful northern cardinal. The other species I've seen, places I've gone birdwatching—most important, birders I've met—it all started when I was just a little kid who liked a bird with red feathers.

Nate Koszycki *Toledo, Ohio*

House Wren

With a melodious song like no other and a feisty spirit, the bird that first won my heart was the house wren, which my mother affectionately called the "Jenny wren." Growing up, we had teapot birdhouses with very small openings to accommodate these busy little fliers, and each spring we watched as they worked tirelessly to build stick nests. To this day, house wrens still call my backyard home. So much so that one day, my son asked me why I had put sticks in his jeans. It turned out that an industrious wren had begun to build a nest in his jeans while they were drying on the line outside. I had just folded them up without noticing, sticks and all!

Boni Trombetta *West Chester, Pennsylvania*

A colorful northern cardinal pushed one young birder to keep exploring the world of birds.

Birding is a family's new hobby thanks to an American redstart.

American Redstart

I grew up with a love of nature, but it wasn't until my mid-20s that I really fell for the birds. It happened during my second year at the Biggest Week in American Birding in northwest Ohio. The first time I went, it was primarily to people-watch. The second time was part of a camping trip with my then-girlfriend, now-wife. We were riding our bikes along the shoreline when

we spotted a flock of little orange and black birds. They looked like miniature orioles, but I knew they had to be something else—so we looked them up in a field guide. They were American redstarts, a type of warbler.

My wife and I both thought that was pretty neat, and we ended up going to one of the festival's "birder socials" hosted by *Birds & Blooms,* where we were invited to go birding on the Magee Marsh boardwalk

the next day. With just one pair of binoculars between us, we headed to the boardwalk, where one of our new birding friends introduced us to all the unusual birds flitting through the trees.

We now plan a camping trip to Biggest Week each spring. It all started with a small warbler, and it led to a new passion and some great friendships.

Patrick Hogan *Temperance, Michigan*

BOOKS WE LOVE

Go deeper into more life-changing bird stories when you read these selections.

- Noah Strycker takes off on a globe-trotting adventure to see as many bird species as he can in his memoir *Birding Without Borders.*

- At age 16, Kenn Kaufman went on the ultimate birding road trip. He shares the story of his impressive quest in *Kingbird Highway: The Biggest Year in the Life of an Extreme Birder.*

- In *Birds Art Life: A Year of Observation,* Kyo Maclear discovers the world of birds living in her city of Toronto. This meditative book includes the author's illustrations.

YEAR-ROUND COLOR
When male painted buntings migrate to warm regions for the winter, they keep their rainbow plumage instead of molting into drab colors.

Rainbows *in the Sky*

You have to see this prismatic feeder bird to believe it.

YOU RECOGNIZE COMMON FEEDER BIRDS by color. Red? Cardinal. Blue? Blue jay. Yellow? Goldfinch. But when all those colors and more are on one bird, you're looking at a painted bunting.

Males have bright blue heads, red bodies and yellow-green backs, with darker green on the wings. They develop this bold color in the fall of their second year. Females and juveniles sport a lime green hue, an unusual color among North American feeder birds.

Look for painted buntings in the south central and southeastern states. They have two distinct summer breeding areas. One covers a large area from Texas to Mississippi and north to Kansas, and another is centered in the coastal Carolinas. Painted buntings undertake a short winter migration to Florida, Mexico and Central America, when they gather in small mixed flocks with other birds, such as their indigo bunting cousins.

During their breeding season, males are extremely territorial. They stake out an area of about 3 to 8 acres and defend it vigorously from other males. Vicious fights may ensue, with males wounding other males. Females may even get caught up in the fray. Once the territory is secure, males sing and spread their feathers to attract a mate. Together they choose a nest site, generally in dense vegetation about 3 to 6 feet off the ground.

Females build the nests and lay a clutch of three or four pale eggs speckled with brown, which they incubate alone for about 11 days. Once the eggs hatch, the female stays busy feeding her young brood, again with no help from her mate. The hatchlings fledge the nest in about nine days, and females often lay a second clutch of eggs soon after.

For most of the year, painted buntings are seed-eaters, favoring seed from native grasses like switchgrass. During the breeding season, they switch to protein-heavy insects for extra energy. Females may steal bugs caught in spiderwebs, and even pull webs down to feast on the spiders that built them. Once breeding

Female or young male painted bunting (the two are nearly identical)

season ends, they return to seeds, especially ones they find on or near the ground.

To attract these stunning fliers to your yard, offer millet seed in a feeder with perches. Painted buntings are wary and easily scared off, so hang a feeder with a protective cage around the tube to discourage bully birds. Ensure that your yard provides low dense vegetation by planting plenty of native grasses. These bright beauties love birdbaths, too.

Patience is the key with painted buntings. They may be slow to come around, but once they find a constant food source and protective shelter, they're likely to return frequently.

Prairie warbler

Using Their *Senses*

Discover the fascinating ways birds survive through sight, sound, taste, touch and smell.

Great horned owl

Male and female mockingbirds look the same to humans, but heightened vision allows these birds to see gender differences.

FINCHES, SPARROWS AND CARDINALS are happily filling up at your backyard feeders. All of a sudden, they fly away fast, diving into the bushes. Less than a minute later, a hawk swoops through the yard. How did the songbirds know the hawk was coming? Did they smell, or maybe hear, it? To figure this out, it helps to know more about the senses that birds use to experience the world around them.

Bird's-Eye View

The term "eagle-eyed" for sharp vision is no accident. Nearly all birds see at least two or three times as much detail as humans, making them able to spot food—or approaching predators— that much farther away. Most birds also have excellent color vision. For night birds like owls there may be a biological trade-off: They see very well in dim light, but their perception of colors may not be as good.

Another advantage birds have is seeing ultraviolet light. To humans, male and female northern mockingbirds look exactly the same, but birds are able to tell the difference because the two have different ultraviolet markings.

This long-eared owl is named for the tufts on its head. They look like ears, but they're just feathers, and they may help to camouflage the owl by breaking up its outline.

Because their eyes are on the sides of their heads, most birds take in two separate pictures of their world, one on each side, and have only a limited area of two-eyed vision toward the front. That means while they see lots of detail, it's harder for them to judge distance on the sides until they move their heads.

And birds' eyes process information much faster than human eyes. When you watch a film, the projector may show 24 frames every second, but your eyes blend them together so you see smooth, continuous motion on the screen. For a bird, the same film would look like a quick series of separate pictures. This rapid visual judgment is very helpful for a bird zooming among tree branches, for example.

Hear This

They're not visible, but the ears of birds are located on the sides of their heads, with openings below and behind the eyes, hidden by feathers.

Hearing is critical to bird survival. They need acute hearing to communicate, recognize their young in large nesting colonies, and listen for predators and sometimes prey. Owls have special adaptations for the latter task—ears that are situated asymmetrically, with one slightly lower

than the other. This helps them to detect more precisely where a sound is coming from, so they can hunt successfully even in the more complete darkness of night.

While the tufts of some owls may look like ears, they're really just feathers. Even the shape of feathers on faces helps with hearing, with facial discs that funnel sound back to their ears.

Birds' ears, just like their eyes, can take in information very quickly. If you record a simple birdcall and slow it down, you will discover all kinds of details there that your ears didn't discern. Other birds probably can hear these extra sounds—otherwise there would be no reason for the birds to make them.

Touch and Go

Birds use their sense of touch in a variety of ways, including feeding and flying. They have highly sensitive touch receptors in areas such as their feet, bills and tongues. Some shorebirds feed almost exclusively by touch. As they probe the mud, concentrated touch receptors in bills allow them to detect and gobble up prey hidden below the surface.

Woodpeckers use sensors in their tongues to detect grubs and other food items. Birds also use touch to sense slight changes in air pressure, adjusting their wings accordingly. There are no nerve endings in the feathers themselves, but there are sensitive nerves where the feathers grow from the skin.

A Matter of Taste (and Smell)

Birds have far fewer taste buds than humans do, so their sense of taste may not be as well developed, but no one knows for sure. Scientists have learned that hummingbirds can judge how much sweetness is in nectar or sugar water. And most birds will quickly spit out caterpillars that contain bitter chemicals.

People once believed that birds had very little sense of smell, but advanced research is changing that idea. For example, turkey vultures find carrion by smell, and seabirds that wander the ocean catch a faint whiff of food from far away. In fact, many birds may be able to detect some scents. But it's probable that on average, their sense of smell isn't much better than a human's.

Overall, birds experience their world in many of the same ways that we do, with a focus on sight and sound—but with some fascinating differences, too.

At feeding time, a Wilson's snipe uses touch receptors in its long bill to locate worms and other invertebrates underground.

A SIXTH SENSE

In addition to their five senses, birds have one other amazing ability— they sense the Earth's magnetic field. This ability to judge north and south is clearly helpful as they navigate the sky, especially in migration seasons. Scientists are still figuring out how they do it, but the latest clues suggest that magnetic detection is based in certain proteins in their eyes. In a way, birds may be "seeing" the magnetic field.

Turkey vultures use their sense of smell to locate carrion, the most important part of their diet.

Meet the Thrushes

From robins to bluebirds, this group of shy singers comes in several sizes and colors. Know which is which the next time a thrush visits your backyard.

HERMIT THRUSH

Similar in appearance to a Swainson's thrush, the hermit has a more reddish tail. In cold weather, it's the most common brown thrush to see. Its color varies by region: warmer brown in the East, grayer in the Rockies.

SWAINSON'S THRUSH

A speckled chest, slim body, pale eye-ring and short straight bill means you're looking at a Swainson's thrush. Its call is a soft *hwoit*.

WOOD THRUSH
To identify a wood thrush, keep an eye out for black spots on a white chest, and brown back feathers that transition to reddish hues on the head.

FOR MOST BACKYARD BIRDERS, thrushes tend to fly under the radar. But you may be more familiar with this varied group than you realize. Although they may not look it, American robins and bluebirds are both part of the same family of thrushes.

More than two dozen species of thrushes have been observed in North America. Many of them are rare, strong-flying strays that have wandered far from Europe, Asia or the tropics. But several common types of native thrushes are well-worth looking for, too.

Brown Thrushes

Six species of thrushes with brown backs and spotted chests live in forests across North America. They sing from the trees but do most of their feeding on the ground, hopping and running in the shadows. And what they lack in bright colors, they more than make up for with the beauty of their songs.

Most brown thrush species live in the far north or in high mountains during summer. The wood thrush is found all over the eastern states, in forests or in backyards with lots of trees and thickets. It's the largest species of this thrush group (but still smaller than an American robin) and the one with the boldest black spots on its chest. The foxy reddish brown of its head and upper back is hard to notice when it loiters in deep shade. Wood thrushes sometimes venture to the edges of lawns, making them much easier to spot. Like most of their relatives, wood thrushes migrate to the tropics for the winter.

The only brown thrush you're likely to see in the cold months is the hermit thrush. Some stay through the winter all across the southern states, from California to the Carolinas, and a few as far north as the Great Lakes. This thrush also migrates later in fall and earlier in spring than its relatives. Spot its reddish brown tail, contrasting with a dull brown back. When the hermit thrush pauses in the open, it may raise and lower its tail while flicking its wings out to the side in a nervous-appearing motion.

TOWNSEND'S SOLITAIRE

Find this thrush in forest edges in the West. The white eye-ring and long, slim tail with white outer feathers are key marks to look for in the field.

A CHORUS OF BROWN THRUSHES

Accomplished singers, thrushes deliver some of the most beautiful bird songs in North America.

WOOD THRUSH: a rich, deep fluting whistle (*ee-oh-lay*).

HERMIT THRUSH: one long, clear note and then a short, quick warbling phrase.

SWAINSON'S THRUSH: a short, low note followed by whistled phrases; at the end a higher note.

VEERY: breezy whistles that spiral down in pitch (*veeyurr, veeyurr, veeyurr*).

GRAY-CHEEKED THRUSH: whistled phrases with a nasal tone (*veeyer, vidi veer, de veer*).

BICKNELL'S THRUSH: like the gray-cheeked thrush but thinner; ends on a higher note.

Townsend's Solitaire

When you walk through open juniper woods in the West in winter, listen for a small bell ringing in the distance. This is the callnote of Townsend's solitaire, a slim gray thrush with a bold white eye-ring. Solitaires are usually seen alone, as their name suggests, perching bolt upright in the open. They fly out to catch insects in midair or flutter down to pick them from foliage. In cold weather, they eat mostly berries. For the summer, most solitaires move to the higher mountains. They build their nests on the ground, well-hidden under logs or in the protected spots among rocks.

Varied Thrush

At first glance, it's easy to mistake this thrush for a robin. A chunky, shorter-tailed bird, it's more shy than its robin cousin. This bird hides in dense forest cover, where it can be hard to see, but it's worth the effort to try to get a good look. The varied thrush has a striking pattern, with an orange eyebrow, complicated orange wing stripes and a dark band across the chest.

Varied thrushes are most common in the Pacific Northwest. In summer, they live in cool evergreen forests from southern Alaska to Idaho and northwestern California. Males perch in treetops to sing a long breathy note that sounds as if they're both whistling and humming at the same time.

For winter, most varied thrushes move south in the Pacific Coast states, though a few go off-course and fly to the east. Wandering varied thrushes have been seen in almost every eastern state and all along the Atlantic Coast, from southern Canada to Florida. Such a surprising visitor could show up anywhere. Make sure you take a second look at every robin that visits your backyard. It just might be a varied thrush!

RIGHT AT HOME

Look for the western tanager's bright flame-colored feathers nestled within evergreen branches. Tree canopies are its most frequented habitat.

Fiery Fliers

Western conifer forests light up when these glowing tanagers arrive.

BIRDERS IN THE WEST are in the right area but may need luck to spot the flashy feathers of western tanagers. With bright red heads, vibrant yellow bodies, and black wings and tails, males resemble a bright flickering flame. Females and young males are less showy, sporting muted yellow bodies with black wings. Despite the bold field marks, these tanagers are hard to find, often hiding in the treetops of western conifer forests.

"Western tanagers are more often heard than seen at our place," says Sally Roth, lifelong naturalist and author who lives amid a dense pine and spruce forest in the high Rockies of northern Colorado.

"When I hear one singing, I lift up my binoculars to find it," Sally says. "That color is unmistakable! It sure catches your eye against the green of the trees."

As western tanagers arrive from Mexico and Central America during spring migration, they seek extra fuel in backyard offerings of dried and fresh fruit, especially orange halves.

Sally sees one or two western tanagers at her feeders each spring. "But once they claim their nesting territory, they aren't interested in the feeder—there are too many tasty caterpillars around," she says.

Like orioles, western tanagers consume mostly insects once breeding season begins. Protein-packed grasshoppers, wasps, ants, termites and beetles are favorites. The birds nab bugs while in flight or carefully pluck them from foliage, branches and flowers as they forage through trees and shrubs.

The male western tanager is extremely protective over his breeding area. He belts out a robinlike song, full of rising and falling whistles, to stake his claim. Meanwhile, a female scouts out a nesting site almost as soon as she arrives at the breeding grounds. She swiftly flies through open tree canopies until she finds a suitable spot to raise a family.

Nest-building duties are the female's job, although the male is never far away. Four or five days after she begins building, the pair has a

Female western tanager

brand-new twig home that is filled in and lined with various materials such as bark, moss, stems, grasses, pine needles and feathers.

A backyard filled with trees is the best way to encourage western tanagers to call your landscape home or stop by for a quick snack. When they're passing through during fall migration, fruits like serviceberry, blackberry and elderberry help to fill them up.

Birdbaths, especially those with moving water, lure western tanagers and many other species throughout summer and during spring and fall migrations.

A Sudden *Surge* of Birds

Keep a close eye on your feeders this winter. Hungry, nomadic fliers from the far north may make an unexpected stop.

REDPOLLS IN TEXAS, white-winged crossbills in the Great Plains, and snowy owls scattered like confetti across the continent. When you hear of these unexpected sightings, it means one thing—it's an irruption year. An irruptive migrant is a species that usually migrates short distances at the most, but occasionally moves far south in very large numbers. The reason for these unique migrations is not straightforward, and researchers have found that the causes vary with the species.

In the winter of 2012, an abundance of boreal songbirds headed south out of their normal range. Bohemian waxwings, pine siskins, red-breasted nuthatches, crossbills, redpolls, pine and evening grosbeaks all appeared in unusual places.

The sudden boom began in the spring, which was an unusually cool and rainy one. With those weather conditions, pine and spruce trees in the boreal forest produced fewer cones, the main food for northern songbirds. And as the winter approached, their fare became scarce, and the desperate birds headed south in search of more productive foraging.

Steven Matsuoka, a research wildlife biologist for the U.S. Geological Survey in Anchorage, Alaska, described the activity of these birds as

When food in the northern conifer forest is scarce, pine grosbeaks head south.

resource tracking. "The birds are essentially going where there is food," he said. "It's part of what makes these species hard to study—they are constantly moving."

While each species has its own threshold for an irruptive migration, in most years at least one species makes the journey. Although it happened in 2012, it's rare for conditions to push many types of birds south at once.

Northern owls like snowies, great grays, boreals, saw-whets and northern hawk owls have different reasons for heading south.

"Some owls have irruptive migrations due to a lack of food, while others move because abundant food has led to high productivity," said Scott Weidensaul, one of the founders of Project SNOWstorm, a research effort to study snowy owls. "Boreal forest owls tend to be the first, and snowy owls tend to be the second."

Northern hawk owls, boreal owls and great gray owls fly south when food, such as voles and lemmings, is scarce. Like the cone-dependent songbirds, they move out of their northern homes to find food. But snowies and saw-whets appear in the largest numbers when the populations of small mammals are up.

According to Scott, when lots of small mammals are around, snowy owls are very productive nesters. Broods of chicks are large and easily fed, and due to the abundant food, most of the youngsters survive the normally dangerous first weeks away from the nest. When snow arrives, draping the hunting grounds in a deep layer of fluff, all of those tasty lemmings and voles are suddenly much less accessible, and there is a lot of competition for good hunting grounds. The young birds, unequipped to cope with these hardships, irrupt south, in search of something better.

SONGBIRDS THAT IRRUPT

Black-capped and boreal chickadee

Bohemian and cedar waxwing

Common and hoary redpoll

Clark's nutcracker

Evening and pine grosbeak

Pine siskin

Purple finch

Red-breasted nuthatch

Red and white-winged crossbill

Reports of Bohemian
waxwing sightings
at *ebird.org* were
above average in the
winter of 2016-17.

During irruptive years, backyard birders in the Lower 48 may see evening grosbeaks.

FEED THE NORTHERNERS

When hungry irruptive species arrive in your yard, serve their favorites.

REDPOLLS AND SISKINS
Food: Thistle (Nyjer)
Feeder: Tube or mesh feeders

PINE AND EVENING GROSBEAKS
Food: Black oil sunflower seed
Feeder: Tray or tube feeder with perches

NUTHATCHES
Food: Suet and peanut butter
Feeder: Mesh block for suet, and simply spread peanut butter on tree trunks and branches

As biologists hash out the different causes of irruptive migrations, they are also learning how to predict them.

Project FeederWatch, administered in the U.S. by the Cornell Lab of Ornithology, describes itself as "a winter-long survey of birds that visit feeders at backyards, nature centers, community areas, and other locales in North America." Emma Greig, project leader there, said, "By looking at feeder count data in past years, we can clearly see when irruptive migrations have occurred. From there we can look at the climate and weather conditions and see what those years may have had in common."

By analyzing that data across the north over time, it's possible to determine which species, if any, are likely to appear further south the following winter. The trouble, however, is that the arctic and boreal forests are vast regions with a lot of variability from one part to another. What is happening in Alaska may not reflect what's going on in eastern Canada. Those who study this phenomenon admit that irruptive migrations are still not fully understood.

So, as a birder, it's important to always keep your eyes open, especially in the winter. You just might see that one really desirable species.

Sometimes very
elusive, great gray
owls unexpectedly
wander outside
their range.

PHOTOS *of the* YEAR

Enjoy these gorgeous shots from the past year of *Birds & Blooms* magazine. Go to *birdsandblooms.com/ submit* to contribute.

1 Barred owl
Laurie Painter
SILVER CLIFF, WISCONSIN

2 Cedar waxwing
Frank Rodin
SARNIA, ONTARIO

3 Sandhill cranes
Allen Bosch
VENICE, FLORIDA

2

3

Attracting
BIRDS

Lure a variety of desirable species to your yard with these simple pointers.

CHAPTER 2

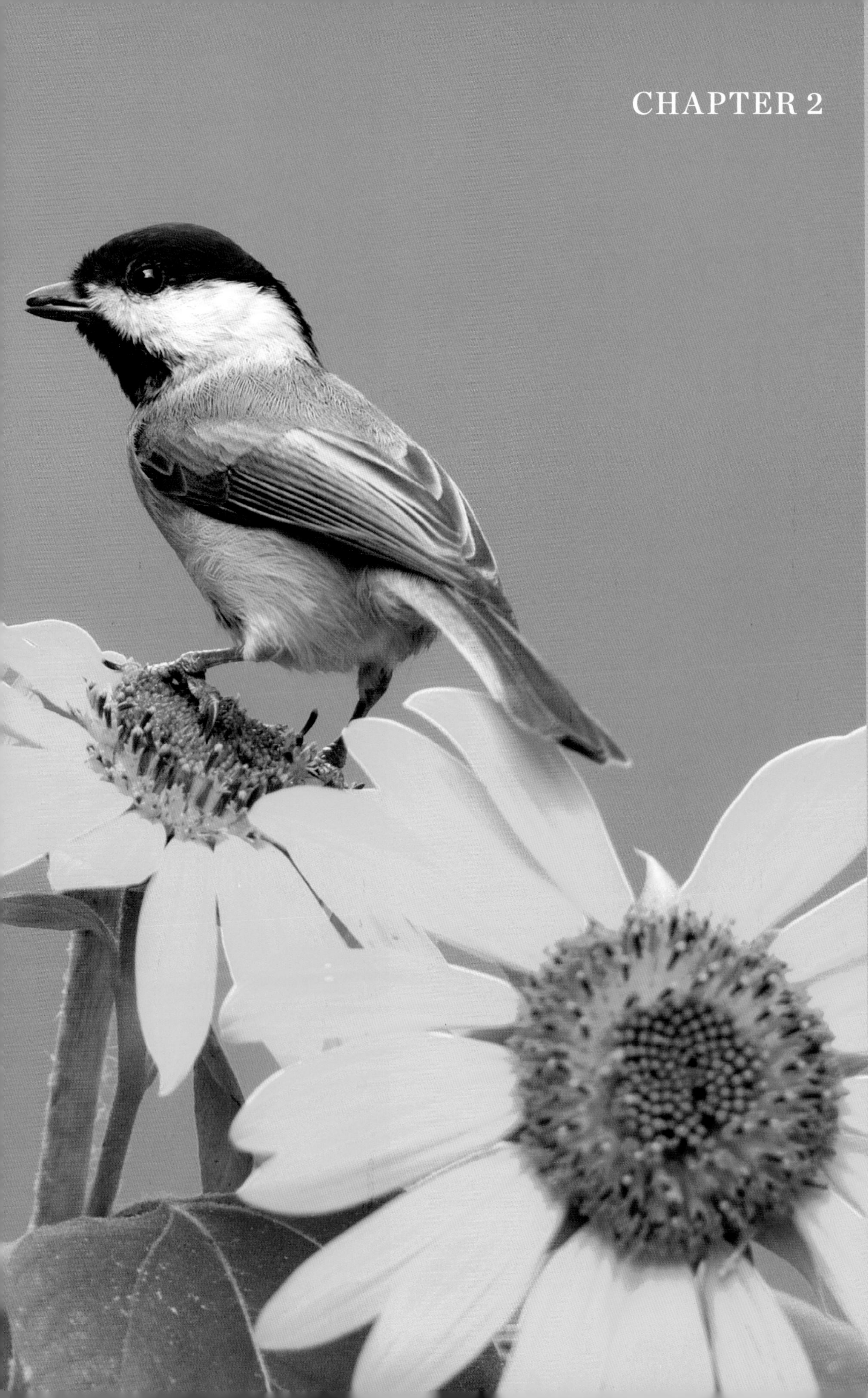

Birdscape Your Backyard

Create a garden that gives your favorite fliers plenty of natural places to hide.

BEYOND THE FLURRY OF ACTIVITY at the feeder, there's a never-ending performance happening throughout your bird-friendly garden. It's the way birds position themselves within your space when they are not at the feeder, rapidly moving from limb to branch, ground to tree, and back again. These behaviors, a way to ensure survival, offer hours of fascinating observation.

A bird's sole life purpose is to produce offspring, so all of its movements are driven by natural instincts to find food, water, shelter, protection and safe nesting sites. Backyard habitats offering sufficient variety and quantity of shrubbery, trees and structures provide those life essentials.

Rhiannon Crain, project leader of the Cornell Lab of Ornithology's Habitat Network (*yardmap.org*), says birds are attracted to "three different layers of habitat: overstory, midstory and understory." Birds have "evolved to be in those

HIDING PLACES

The most bird-friendly landscapes have plants at every level, from the ground to the treetops, to give birds plenty of places to hide from predators. Use trees, shrubs, vines and ground covers that thrive in different seasons.

American goldfinch

locations in the yard," Rhiannon says. "When developing a bird-friendly backyard habitat, many think only in a one-dimensional way—looking down at a landscape plan. Often they don't think about critical layered areas for birds."

An array of trees and shrubs in different sizes and shapes makes life easier and more energy-efficient for birds because they can quickly and casually hide among branches or fade into shadows in the foliage when a threat is near. "Birds like different levels of vegetation to accommodate their niches," Rhiannon says.

BEHAVIORS WORTH KNOWING
Birds use trees, shrubs and plants to perform these evasive and defensive maneuvers.

Bird plow: pushing collectively toward predator

Hook: flying up and around, only far enough to be out of danger

Popcorn: popping up and out of the way, up or down to mirror predator movements

Parabolic/Umbrella: encircling and following predator through territory

Bullet: racing ahead of aerial predator

Ditch/Hawk drop: dropping down from upper branches into denser cover

Pick up a copy of Jon Young's book What the Robin Knows *for more information on defensive behaviors and alarm calls.*

Some birds may know even more details about your backyard than you do, such as the best hiding places and shelters, and the known dangers lurking there.

In his book, *What the Robin Knows,* author Jon Young observes that a bird's movement within a landscape is based on energy-saving tactics. Most fliers know a recognized predator's reach, and in order to conserve valuable energy, they retreat to what Jon refers to as their "just far enough" distance for safety.

Birds tend to "move through the landscape only as far as necessary when recognizing a specific threat, reacting as necessary," Jon writes. "Ground birds that know a particular cat can jump only 4 feet off the ground will ascend to a branch 5 feet up—why go 20 feet up when 5 feet is sufficient?"

A variety of dense foliage from ground level to the upper tree canopy creates pathways and corridors to let birds travel safely throughout your yard. "Birds don't like to cross open spaces," Rhiannon says. "They will go 10 times as far so as not to cross an open area."

Herb Lewis, an Alabama Master Gardener, lives within a flyway along the Tennessee River Valley and studies bird behavior in his lush and diverse yard, a Certified Wildlife Habitat. "To build density from the ground up into the trees and higher elevations, I would use flowering shrubbery," Herb says. "In the spring and summer months, use a lot of annuals—they work really well on the ground level."

All of this plant cover might seem beneficial to predators as well, but Herb says that overall it works in the bird's favor. "The birds don't come out long enough for a predator to attack them," he says.

Landscapes that offer a wide variety of food sources—fruit, seeds and insects—at different times throughout the year make the most inviting and bird-friendly habitat. Expand the environment beyond your own backyard by coordinating your plantings and corridors with your neighbors.

"It's important to build a garden for beauty, but also for bird conservation and habitat," Herb says. Follow Herb's lead and certify your backyard habitat with the National Wildlife Federation (*nwf.org/certify*).

PREVIOUS SPREAD: ADAM GIBBS/KAC PRODUCTIONS; THIS SPREAD, CLOCKWISE FROM TOP LEFT: INGRID MATHEWS; TINA PATTERSON; BERNICE PLUM; LESLEY RITTER

Rose-breasted grosbeak

THE BIG THREE
Food, water and shelter are key. Birds love the seeds from sunflowers (far left) and coneflowers in addition to feeder seed. Birdbaths and houses also make your yard more desirable.

American robin nest

Eastern bluebird

What Warblers Want

Entice these colorful migrants to your backyard with the essentials they need to thrive—food, water and shelter.

A SMALL BIRD DARTS through the dense brush. Its striking field marks—bold stripes of yellow and black—make it look too tropical to be in northern North America. The warbler dodges in and out of the branches, gleaning an insect here and there or stopping to belt out a loud, twittering song. Warblers like this yellow-rumped warbler are constantly on the move, favor thick cover and can be frustratingly difficult to observe.

More than 50 species of wood warblers flit and fly around North America. From Alaska to the mangroves of Florida, they are found just about everywhere. Some parts of the country are blessed with more than two dozen species, while other locales have only a few. Most of the warblers you see are seasonal visitors, migrating from their breeding grounds in the U.S. and Canada to wintering areas in South and Central America.

Because of habitat loss, free-ranging cats and other changes brought by human communities, many warbler species have suffered steep

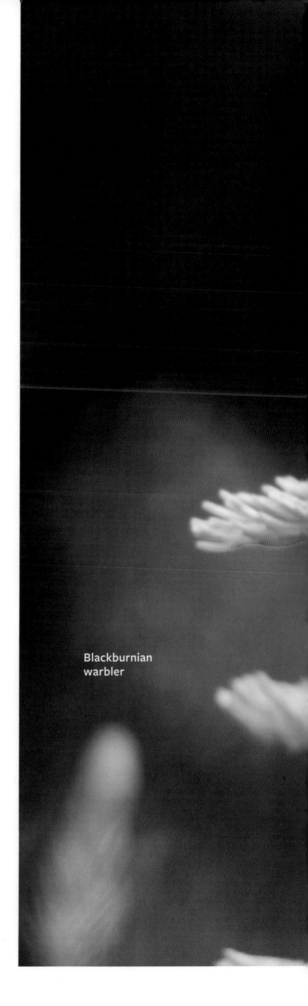

Blackburnian warbler

population declines. Fortunately for warbler lovers, there's a crucial tool to help these flashy migrants—your landscape. Plan it to provide the environment they require to thrive, including the right food, inviting water and a variety of plant life arranged to give plenty of shelter.

Food

Unlike sparrows, orioles, finches, chickadees and other common species, warblers are infrequent visitors to backyard bird feeders. Most are strict insectivores, so you won't entice these colorful fliers with the typical menu of seeds. Yet despite their disinterest in feeders, you can still attract warblers to your yard.

Some species, like yellow-rumped warblers, occasionally visit feeders for a morsel of black oil sunflower, suet or peanut butter. And orange halves may draw in just a few more.

But since most warblers forgo feeding stations, make sure your yard is providing the food they love most: insects.

Plants you prize for their color and texture are magnets for small insects. However, the timing of blossoming has to be right. Since warblers in much

Common yellowthroat

of North America are seasonal, "growing plants that are in fruit or flower when warblers are around is the key to providing food," says Geoff Geupel, director of the emerging programs and partnerships group at Point Blue Conservation Science in California. "You've got to sync up the plants with the birds." This can make creating an attractive space for warblers in your backyard a little bit challenging.

In fall and winter, warblers will eat berries, like this black-throated blue snacking on beautyberry.

A prothonotary warbler snatches up an insect to eat.

A NATURAL PESTICIDE

Insects are crucial to a warbler's diet, and they have to eat a lot of them. From mosquitoes to aphids, these birds consume many kinds of pests. Providing habitat for warblers in your yard not only will make your garden a more colorful place, but it will also help reduce the pests!

WARBLERS AND BEYOND

A safe and desirable habitat is attractive to more than just warblers. If you build it, other backyard favorites that shy away from feeders may stop by, too:

- Bluebirds
- Owls
- Phoebes
- Robins
- Tanagers
- Thrashers
- Thrushes
- Vireos
- Waxwings
- Wrens

Increase your chances of attracting a yellow warbler by providing backyard shelter, like trees and shrubs.

Magnolia warbler

Warblers, like this yellow-throated, love backyard water features.

When planning a garden, put your best naturalist skills to work. Determine the time of year that warblers are in your area. Go birding often, or use online tools such as eBird (*ebird.org*) to determine when local warblers are present. Then select plant species that bloom or fruit at the same time.

Water

Warblers love water. While out birding, you'll find some of the best places to observe these species are along small creeks and streams. But it can be tricky to lure warblers to your space with a birdbath that contains only still water.

Flowing or moving water is much more enticing. Add a bubbler or fountain, or create a tiny artificial stream to lure thirsty warblers in for a drink or a quick bath. An ornamental creek that provides some natural splashing sounds is ideal. Include swift areas, shallows and little waterfalls to make your yard come alive with birds and the pleasing sounds of tumbling water.

Habitat

Warblers need a wide range of natural spaces, so providing different habitats in your landscape is a sure way to invite more than one species. "The more diversity in your yard, the better," Geoff says. It's not complicated, but varied habitat structures may be the most important part of the warbler-attracting formula.

Some species, such as Townsend's warblers, spend their time in the tops of trees, while others, like yellow and mourning warblers, prefer dense shrubs. Take a moment or two to envision your garden in a vertical cross section. Tall trees provide habitat for canopy species, while a layer of thick shrubs offers a safe spot for warblers that prefer dense cover. Close to the ground, a layer of low shrubs and annuals makes a safe foraging area. Even a simple brush pile in the corner of the yard can offer a resting spot away from free-roaming cats and other predators.

Geoff emphasizes native plants. "I think native vegetation is hugely important," he says. "Native plants are more resilient and longer-lived than introduced species, and they create better habitat for birds."

When your landscape contains abundant resources found in a natural ecosystem (food, water and sheltering habitat structures), it becomes an oasis for birds and other wildlife. A bird-filled backyard is your reward for actively protecting these colorful migrants.

13 Ways to Be a Bird's *Best Friend*

Readers share tried-and-true advice for transforming backyards into bustling bird havens.

1. Water, food and shelter

are essential. Any one of them is a solid start, but combine all three and more birds than ever will call your backyard home. Then, the next step is to vary your feeders by location, seed type and height. Once you switch up the feeders, sit back in a comfy chair under the shade and enjoy the show.
Kathy Eppers, Aledo, Texas

2. If you're new to watching

birds, pick up an illustrated field guide and keep it near a window that looks out on your feeders. I keep my copy of *Birds of North America* from St. Martin's Press near my favorite window— it's always there when I need it. Once you learn to recognize the common species in your neighborhood, research what their preferred foods are so you can attract even more to your space.
Sydra Krueger, Bay City, Michigan

Carolina chickadee on sunflowers

MMM, BERRIES! A yellow-breasted chat gets a calorie boost from a beautyberry shrub.

3. Different foods attract

different birds, so make sure you're offering as wide a variety as possible. For example, right now, I am serving thistle for the goldfinches, sugar water for the hummingbirds, jelly for the orioles and several types of high-fat suet blocks for the woodpeckers.
Roberta Klein, Byron, New York

4. Birds really love water

plus it's a necessity, especially in winter. My neighborhood fliers are drawn in by the sound of splashing water from the waterfall in my backyard pond. I also have several heated birdbaths. In the warmer months, it's important to grow natural, blooming food sources that do more than just beautify your space. I use coneflower, sunflower, beautyberry, native honeysuckle vine, bee balm and milkweed in my bird-friendly garden.

I supplement with seed mixes, nuts and a lot of suet, which really draws in the woodpeckers.
Boni Trombetta, West Chester, Pennsylvania

5. Protect the backyard birds

you attract by always keeping pet cats indoors. It's better for the overall health of your beloved cats, too!
Judy Roberts, Graytown, Ohio

6. Think outside the box

and reuse what you can. For example, my feeders are in an area with little cover. In January, I go to my local public works department where people dispose of their Christmas trees. I find some really full ones and place them around my feeders for shelter during the rough winter months to come. (I check for any leftover and potentially harmful decorations or hooks first.) It's a great way to recycle old Christmas trees.
Patty Dorsey, North Huntingdon, Pennsylvania

MAKE IT MOVE
Entice more fliers with
a fountain or a dripper
in your birdbath.

7. Tall shrubs

(about 10 to 15 feet high) invite birds like robins and cardinals to build their nests in the safety of the dense foliage. Your new bird neighbors will be in a more secure space and farther away from predators. After a pair of robin parents settled into our backyard bushes, they flitted around to look for worms to feed their young.

Sharon Blumberg, Munster, Indiana

8. Bugs, bugs, bugs and more

bugs. For the sake of insect-eaters, which include grosbeaks, hummingbirds and bluebirds, skip the pesticides and embrace the bugs. Hungry neighborhood birds help naturally control insect populations in your backyard. Many bird species switch to insects almost exclusively while feeding their nestlings because the young need so much protein. And be sure to leave up spider webs when you see them—hummingbirds use the silky webs to build their nests.

Jill Staake, Tampa, Florida

9. One simple way to help

mother birds is to leave out eggshells, which give them a calcium boost. Every night I eat an egg for supper, then rinse out the shell to let it dry. I break it up a bit and leave it outside my kitchen door for the birds to peck at in the morning. The blue jays especially seem to love it!

Roger Emerick, South Glastonbury, Connecticut

Mealworms are a bluebird's favorite meal.

10. It's important to keep all

bird feeders clean, but sugar-water feeders are especially tricky. I was frustrated by how hard it was to clean around the tiny feeder ports. In a moment of inspiration, I grabbed my old electric toothbrush, put in fresh batteries and had a blast getting all the gunk out from around those itty-bitty feeder holes. After my initial cleaning spree, I used a permanent marker to officially label my new "bird brush." I've been using it for months.
Liza Marie, Santa Rosa, California

11. Leave the bushes bushy

to provide shelter for birds. Consider putting up branches and perches near the feeders to act as "waiting rooms" for those times when all the feeder slots and perches are taken.
Sue Cassidy, Hughesville, Maryland

12. Provide lots of shelter

that includes shrubs and trees, and feed black oil sunflower seeds or a black-oil heavy mix. I feed the birds in both squirrel-proof and nonsquirrel-proof feeders so even those backyard critters get to eat.
Grace Huffman, Oklahoma City, Oklahoma

13. Research native plants

and trees. I grow a lot of native flowers, and after they finish blooming, their heads offer seeds that goldfinches and other seed-loving birds can't resist. The same idea applies with berry trees. Cardinals and cedar waxwings are sure to stop by for a sweet berry snack. If you are patient, attracting birds with your garden will make for many amazing photo opportunities.
Connie Etter, Martinsville, Indiana

PHOTO OP
A berry-filled juniper tree is extra colorful when an eastern bluebird stops by.

Host a *Peanut Party*

Jays, woodpeckers, chickadees, guaranteed! They may bring along some of their friends—tanagers, robins and wrens.

IT'S TRUE. BIRDS GO NUTS for this treat, packed with fat and protein, that is super easy for backyard bird-watchers to serve. Peanuts in almost any form are a lifesaver in the cold depths of winter, but they also will draw a huge crowd year-round.

"Don't underestimate the attractiveness of peanuts in the shell," says Scott Edwards, guest editor of the National Bird-Feeding Society. "Blue jays seem to prefer them this way, and woodpeckers, chickadees and titmice will take them on as well." Peanuts in the shell tempt cardinals, chickadees, mockingbirds and more. Serve them chopped and birds that typically eat soft foods, such as tanagers, wrens, bluebirds and thrashers, come to the peanut feast.

SNACK TIME
An acrobatic white-breasted nuthatch clings to a feeder full of peanuts in the shell.

Raw or roasted? It's a common question, and birds love both. However, "we generally recommend against salted peanuts," says Holly Faulkner, project assistant for Project FeederWatch at the Cornell Lab of Ornithology.

Put out the peanut feeders, and let the bird circus begin!

JAYS. If you've ever attempted to grab a big handful of potato chips, you'll laugh when you watch jays try to do the same with peanuts. Discarding those that don't fit, they stuff as many as possible into their throat pouch and bill. All blue-colored jay species are enthusiastic peanut eaters—and stashers, caching their treasures under tree bark, in crevices or beside rocks to retrieve later.

WOODPECKERS. Every woodpecker, from the adorable downy to the giant pileated, eagerly snatches peanuts to eat on the spot or store for a later day. Whole, chopped or shelled—when it comes to these snacks, they are not picky.

SMALL SONGBIRDS. Chickadees, titmice and nuthatches may be small, but they're among the biggest peanut fans, employing assorted techniques for claiming their crunchy prizes.

FOOD TO GO This blue jay is likely going to stash its peanut away to eat it later.

ALL FIVE
North American titmice—tufted, black-crested, juniper, bridled and oak—stop by feeders for a peanut snack.

OPEN WIDE!
Yes, one of these large peanuts fits in the small bill of a tufted titmouse.

Songbirds are known to hammer the shell, holding it down with their feet. They carry off shelled nuts to stash or eat elsewhere, and they also eagerly devour chopped ones. All of these little gray birds usually take their treats to go, but you can bet they will come back again and again.

NORTHERN CARDINALS. Serve these beauties peanuts out of the shell as whole or half nuts, or chopped. The pyrrhuloxia, the "desert cardinal" of the Southwest, loves this food just as much as its bright red relative.

WRENS. Shelled or chopped peanuts are favored by these perky-tailed birds. If the nuts aren't chopped, wrens work to break off bits. Any species of wren in the neighborhood may visit a peanut feeder, and once a bird finds it, it'll soon be a regular.

NATIVE SPARROWS, JUNCOS, TOWHEES AND DOVES. Keep your eye on the ground beneath peanut feeders, where white-throated, white-crowned, golden-crowned, song and other native sparrows, as well as juncos, towhees and doves, often gather to eagerly peck up the bits that other birds have dropped.

SURPRISE GUESTS. When you serve peanuts, expect the unexpected! Bluebirds, robins, crossbills and other not-so-common feeder birds might visit peanut feeders. "Catbirds, orioles and tanagers happily consume the broken-off pieces from birds pecking the larger nuts," Scott says. So will thrashers, robins, mockingbirds, bluebirds and birds that usually eat insects, fruit and other soft foods.

EASY MEAL It's always fun to watch woodpeckers, like this agile downy, snatch nuts from a cage feeder.

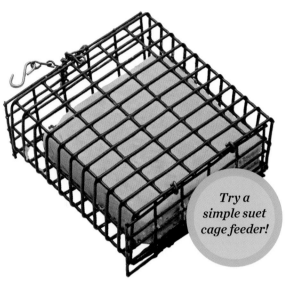

Try a simple suet cage feeder!

Northern flickers love peanuts.

SUET The easiest way to provide suet to birds is to get it straight from your butcher. Put the beef fat in a mesh bag (an empty onion bag works) or a wire cage feeder. If the real deal is a little intense for you, birds will devour premade cakes from the store, too.
Attracts: woodpeckers, chickadees, titmice, jays and nuthatches

PEANUTS Whether you serve peanuts in the shell or out (just avoid the salty kind), put them in a tube or tray feeder. If peanuts get pricey, mix in some black-oil sunflower seeds. In rainy or snowy weather, change out peanuts frequently to prevent mold.
Attracts: jays, woodpeckers, chickadees, nuthatches, titmice and house finches

4 Foods *for Winter*

To attract more birds, add these best-loved options to your backyard menu.

Fill sock feeders with thistle for goldfinches.

THISTLE Fill a mesh tube or sock feeder with thistle (Nyjer) and soon your backyard will be a winter finch haven. The small needlelike seed is a perfect snack for tiny songbirds.
Attracts: goldfinches, pine siskins, house finches and common redpolls

BLACK-OIL SUNFLOWER SEED
A seed preference test performed by the Cornell Lab of Ornithology showed that the majority of feeder birds prefer high-fat black-oil sunflower seed. It's simple to serve, too—spread it right on the snow-covered ground or fill up a tube, tray or hopper feeder.
Attracts: cardinals, grosbeaks, finches, chickadees and nuthatches

SIZE MATTERS
Field Editor Lizzy OeDell of Molalla, Oregon, suggests serving mealworms in a tall, steep dish like this one. The first time she put mealworms out, many of them crawled away!

A Carolina chickadee snatches a mealworm from a feeder.

Mad for
Mealworms

Birds flock to these protein-packed treats.

A BACKYARD FEEDER FULL of nutritious mealworms is beloved by bug-eating birds—and a guaranteed way to spice up your backyard bird feeding routine.

Mealworms are often mistaken for worms, though they're actually the larval form of the mealworm beetle. They are clean, easy to work with, an excellent source of nutrients, and an aid to birds through cold winter weather and spring reproduction.

"The connection that is created between people and nature from feeding birds is undisputable," said Emma Greig, the project leader of Project FeederWatch, a winterlong survey of feeder birds. Emma offers these easy tips to increase your chances of enticing new bird species:

Live or Dried?
You decide. There are pros and cons to each method. Live mealworms are most appealing to birds, though they come at a price and require work to maintain. Dried mealworms are low-cost and convenient, yet they may not be as effective at catching birds' eyes.

Safe Storage
Once you buy a live batch, put them in a shallow plastic container with a 2- to 5-gallon capacity. Cover with a screen or perforated lid for air circulation. Toss in a few apples for moisture, some loose bran and oatmeal. Mealworms are only as nutritious as the food they eat, so feed the larvae well for one to two days before you share them with birds. Place the container in the refrigerator to slow their growth, and keep them in the larval form that birds love.

The Right Placement
Rather than scattering mealworms on the ground, place them on a platform feeder or

rimmed dish to keep them contained. That way, you're less likely to watch the mischievous mealworms crawl away to safety. The feeders should be located near vegetation and away from windows.

Serving Size
Expect to go through about 100 mealworms per day once birds know where to find them. These protein-filled snacks are only a supplement to their diets, so serving more or fewer is OK.

Cost Control
There are many ways to cut costs and make mealworm feeding manageable. Consider making your own feeder, or simply recycle old kitchen pans or dishes. For long-term savings, buy live larvae in bulk from local or online bird food suppliers. Or raise them yourself for a perpetual source. "If folks have the patience for it, I think that's probably a great way to maintain a nice collection of healthy, nutritious mealworms," Emma said. Look for easy to follow guides online.

Offer a *Warm Welcome*

Create safe and cozy spaces for birds to raise their families.

HANG A FEW BIRDHOUSES in your backyard and get ready for a rewarding adventure as you witness the awe-inspiring life cycle of birds.

When birds nest on your property and raise their young, it's so gratifying. "It's the ultimate standard of success," said Robyn Bailey, project leader of the Cornell Lab of Ornithology's NestWatch program. "And it brings a greater diversity of birds to your backyard." Here are a few tips to get you started.

Choose the Right House

Tailor the house to the bird you want to attract. If you're hoping for a nesting songbird, buy a standard nest box with a 1½-inch entrance hole, commonly called a bluebird box. Birdhouses with a smaller hole, about an inch in diameter, are ideal for chickadees and wrens.

The needs of nesting owls are more specific, so use the Right Bird, Right House online interactive tool at *nestwatch.org* to identify the best box.

Also, make sure the box you choose isn't painted on the inside, because the fumes may affect the birds. Natural wood boxes are ideal for birds, and they age well, lasting about 10 to 15 years. Toss in a few wood chips to help certain birds that don't build nests, including kestrels, ducks and owls.

Prepare for Occupants

If the house you buy doesn't have any hanging instructions attached, take a moment to look them up. Birdhouses should hang in the habitats the birds like most. For example, bluebirds prefer boxes in the open with a clear flight path, while wrens choose a home near woody vegetation. Try not to place the house too close to feeders.

To ensure that the home is available to early nesters, put out your box by February if you live in the South, mid-March if you live up north. If you prefer, you can keep it up all year.

Watch for Nests

"It's a common misconception that you shouldn't check on a bird or monitor its nest," Robyn said. "Checking on your occupants is a good way to make sure things are going the way you'd hope."

Moving as nonintrusively as possible, check your birdhouse once or twice a week, keeping visits to less than a minute. If you want to put your data to good use in studying birds, record what you see using the NestWatch website (*nestwatch.org*) or phone app.

Keep it Clean

Each spring and fall, use a paint scraper to scoop nesting materials out of the birdhouse. If it's heavily soiled, wear a mask and wash the house with soap and water.

HOUSE HUNTERS
Different birds have different birdhouse needs. Tree swallows, for example, prefer nest boxes about 5 to 6 feet off the ground.

BEST FOR THE BIRDS
Look for sunflower varieties that will produce an ample supply of seeds for birds to gobble up. Try Mammoth Gray Stripe, Paul Bunyan and Aztec Gold.

Grow Your Own *Birdseed*

Native sunflowers attract beautiful birds, prized pollinators and important insects.

WHETHER YOU'RE ALREADY a dedicated caretaker of backyard feeders or brand-new to birding, it's always a good idea to kick it up a notch! Plant native sunflowers to attract and feed your beloved birds, build a healthier habitat and make your space easy to manage.

"Anybody, anywhere they live, can support the birds they love by growing native plants," says Tod Winston, program manager for the National Audubon Society's Plants for Birds program. Sunflowers are simple, and it doesn't take much for their seeds to take root. Provide them with plenty of sun and a spot in a patio pot, raised bed or garden, and you'll soon have a crop of flourishing flowers.

Start Here

Check out the National Audubon Society's Native Plants Database or consult local native nurseries to select an ideal species. Plant your sunflower seeds in late spring. The soil must be warm and dry, with no possibility of frost.

Sunflower seeds need a soil temperature of about 50 degrees to sprout. Measure with a thermometer or go with your gut. To test the soil moisture, grab a handful and squeeze. The soil is too wet if it sticks together and doesn't crumble. Once conditions are just right, plant the seeds up to 1 inch deep, with about 12 inches between each seed. They will need about six to eight hours of sunlight each day.

Make an Impact

"The more people who plant native plants in their yard, the more resilient birds are going to be in the face of climate change and in the face of continuing loss of habitat," Tod says. He adds that nearly 41 percent of all migratory songbird populations in North America are declining.

Sunflowers also benefit many pollinators, caterpillars and birds. Their compound flower heads are packed with pollen, and these bright beauties host more than 70 species of native moth and butterfly caterpillars. That's a big deal because one nest of Carolina chickadee chicks may eat up to 9,000 caterpillars before fledging. What's more, 90 percent of land birds feed insects to chicks, so it's important to protect those local populations. As a bonus, migrating birds love the seeds because they're high-fat fuel for their journeys south.

Grow Related Natives

If you're seeking some variety to beautify your backyard, consider planting other natives from the aster family, including coneflowers, tickseed and black- and brown-eyed Susans.

SOCIAL BY THE SEASON
During summer breeding season, indigo buntings hunt alone for food within their nesting territory. In winter, they often roost and forage in flocks.

Go For *Indigo*

With a little landscape planning and their favorite seed at your feeder, you can enjoy this bunting's brilliant beauty.

THE SIZE OF A SPARROW but more finchlike in its appearance, an indigo bunting is truly dazzling. But its flashy hue is not really indigo at all. In fact, no bird has a true blue pigment in its feathers. "The color occurs as an interaction of light within a complex feather structure," says nature columnist, birder and author Gary Clark.

It takes a male bunting two years to reach its full iridescent splendor (which he loses every winter as he molts into brownish feathers). In the meantime, younger males sport splotches of brown and other off-color shades, while the females are tan with whitish throats.

Indigo buntings are common across the eastern half of the U.S., where they produce two broods as they are nestled in dense shrubs or low-growing trees during breeding season. They head to the southernmost tip of Florida, Mexico, Central America and the Caribbean to winter. Come spring, they migrate up to 1,200 miles from wintering spots to breeding grounds in areas including Texas and southern Louisiana.

During their first breeding season, young buntings learn to sing. "Males acquire their song by listening to other males in the neighborhood and slightly modifying it for their own song version," Gary says. "It's not a different song they develop, just a variation, as in human melodies where a singer slightly alters the rhythm and harmony of a tune."

Attracting an indigo bunting to your backyard feeder may be challenging even for folks who live within their range and see them most often. According to Gary, buntings visit feeders most during migration but seldom in breeding season.

"Their breeding habitat includes grass and weed fields in woodland areas, where they eat a variety of insects, spiders, fruits and seeds," he says. "Sunflower seeds would be fine for those

that show up in backyards during migration, although in my experience, they eat seed that's fallen on the ground more than at actual feeders."

If you want to tempt them with feeders, though, most backyard birders will have the best luck with black oil and hulled sunflower seeds, thistle, Nyjer and white proso millet. Try setting out a tube feeder or a tray feeder with perches designed for smaller birds.

Perhaps the best way to entice indigo buntings to your backyard is to model it after their ideal habitat. Bushes, hedges, berry-producing shrubs and flowers provide plenty of shelter and natural food sources like buds, berries and seeds. These plants will also attract many insects—beetles, grasshoppers, aphids and cicadas—that indigo buntings like to feast on the most.

Backyard
ESSENTIALS

*Go back to birding and gardening basics
and make your landscape better than ever.*

CHAPTER 3

12
Backyard
Myths *Busted*

Our experts, Kenn and Kimberly Kaufman and Melinda Myers, set the record straight on some of the most common birding and gardening misconceptions.

MYTH 1 Birds eat very little, which is where the phrase "eat like a bird" comes from.

FACT **Kenn and Kimberly:** Some birds eat constantly. When migrants are getting ready for their long flights, they eat so much that they almost double their weight. Baby birds growing in the nest eat even more. A pair of American robins feeding a hungry family deliver 100 to 150 meals a day to the nest, and each baby robin may eat its weight in insects, worms and berries in a day. Imagine a human teenager eating 80 to 90 pounds of cheeseburgers in a single day—that's a better example of someone "eating like a bird."

When's lunch?

MYTH 2
It's dangerous
to eat rhubarb
harvested during
the summer.

FACT Melinda:
Feel free to eat
rhubarb stalks from
spring through fall.
The flavor is best
when harvested the
first eight to 10 weeks
of the season. It's also
better for the plant
to limit harvesting
time—the more leaves
on it, the more energy
the plant produces
and stores for next
year's growth. Be
aware that rhubarb
leaves contain a lot
of oxalic acid, which
is toxic in large
amounts. So don't
eat those.

RHUBARB
leaves grow
as wide as
2 feet!

Unlike most smaller bird species, a mute swan pair often forms a **BOND FOR LIFE.**

MYTH 3 Birds mate for life.

FACT Kenn and Kimberly: Some bird pairs stick together for several years or even as long as they both live. This happens more often with larger species, such as bald eagles and swans, and birds that don't migrate, such as northern cardinals. Even among these birds, however, separations sometimes happen, especially after an unsuccessful nesting season. It's migratory songbirds that are more likely to switch partners from one year to the next. For example, when a pair of gray catbirds return to the same summering area, they wind up with different mates more than half the time.

MYTH 4 Veggies don't need full sun.

FACT Melinda: Vegetables always produce best in full sun. Tomatoes, peppers, broccoli and other plants (like melons) that produce edible flowers and fruits need the most sunlight—eight hours or more. Still, root crops, like beets and radishes, can produce with four to six hours of full sun, and leafy greens get by in partial shade or indirect sunlight. For them, a shady spot keeps things cool and prolongs the harvest.

Female ruby-throated hummingbird

MYTH 5 If I leave my sugar-water feeder up too long in fall, the hummingbirds won't migrate south.

FACT Kenn and Kimberly: Like other birds, hummingbirds have a powerful instinct to migrate that is triggered by things like the length of daylight. They don't wait until the weather turns bad or until food sources disappear. When their instinct tells them to go, even if your yard is full of feeders and flowers, hummingbirds still fly south. Feel free to leave the feeders up as long as there are hummingbirds flitting around.

MYTH 6 Birds can't smell.

FACT Kenn and Kimberly: Scientists used to believe that birds had little or no sense of smell. But research has proven that many birds *can* smell, and they use that sense in important ways. Turkey vultures often locate carrion by smell. Seabirds that fly over the ocean are attracted to the smell of food at the water's surface, and they may use scent to help find their nesting burrows on islands. And kiwis, wandering New Zealand forests at night, use scent to find worms and other food hidden underground.

MYTH 7 Tomatoes ripen faster if you remove most of their leaves and allow sunlight to reach the fruit.

FACT Melinda: The leaves are critical for growing an abundant harvest of ripe tomatoes. They produce energy for plant growth, flowering and fruiting. Fewer leaves mean less energy to support fruit development. Removing the leaves also exposes the fruit to intense rays of the sun, which can burn the plant and create an entryway for disease.

*No worries!
Mom and Dad
are nearby.*

MYTH 8 A baby bird you find on the ground should be rescued.

FACT Kenn and Kimberly: A young bird out of its nest may look like it needs help, but it's best to back off and observe from a distance. More often than not, the parent birds are near. They continue to feed the youngster while it's on the ground, and if given enough space, lead it to safety. Of course, if the fledgling is in immediate danger—in traffic or threatened by prowling pets—move the bird to a safer spot.

MYTH 9 Only the female birds take care of nesting duties.

FACT Kenn and Kimberly: This is true for some birds, like hummingbirds, but the males of most species provide at least some care. For example, a male Baltimore oriole doesn't take part in nest-building or incubation, but after the eggs hatch, he brings almost half the food for the youngsters. A male downy woodpecker does at least half of the work of digging the nest cavity, incubating the eggs and feeding the young. And among spotted sandpipers, the female may lay eggs in the nest and then depart, leaving the male to hatch the eggs and care for the young on his own.

MYTH 10 Items from the kitchen cabinet make better, more natural pesticides than what's sold at garden centers.

FACT Melinda: Just because a common household product is safe to use in the kitchen doesn't mean it's safe in the garden. Many burn the plant instead of attacking the intended insect, disease or weed. Scientists have introduced some eco-friendly pesticides that use plant oils, soaps and other common products. These are effective against pests, yet safe for plants. I highly recommend the books *The Truth About Garden Remedies* and *The Truth About Organic Gardening.* Jeff Gillman, the author, discusses the science and effectiveness of home remedies.

MYTH 11 Grass won't grow under pine and spruce trees, because their needles add acid to the soil.

FACT Melinda: Evergreen needles have minimal impact on soil acidity. The needles make an excellent garden mulch because they conserve moisture, suppress weeds, moderate soil temperature and improve the soil as they decompose. Too much shade and too little water are the real culprits when grass fails to grow under evergreens and other trees. The mass of leaves and needles creates a dense canopy that shades the ground below and prevents much of the rainfall from reaching the plants beneath the trees. Most of the water that does reach the ground is absorbed by tree roots instead of grass.

MYTH 12 If you plant cucumbers next to pumpkins, they cross-pollinate and ruin the harvest.

FACT Melinda: You can plant pumpkins next to other squash, melons and cucumbers. The seeds you buy grow into the desired fruit no matter what is planted next to it. When bees carry pollen from one plant to another, cross-pollination can occur, but it affects the seeds, not the fruit you eat. However, when you save the seeds from the cross-pollinated plants and use them in next year's garden, you may be in for a surprise. The offspring might be a yellow and green acorn squash, yellow-spotted zucchini or even a pumpkin with green warts.

YES!
You can plant cucumbers and pumpkins together.

MOVE OVER, SQUIRRELS!
If this is a common sight in your yard, deter the seed bandits by giving them easy access to nuts and corn far away from your bird feeders.

Squirrel-Proof Strategies

Find new ways to tackle this classic backyard challenge.

MOST BACKYARD BIRDERS are familiar with this scenario. You select the perfect bird feeder, fill it with an ideal blend of seeds and hang it with care. When you come back later, instead of seeing your favorite birds stopping for a snack, you spot two squirrels stealing from your feeders! It's enough to drive anyone nutty. But before you blow a gasket, here are some humane solutions to combat your squirrel problem.

1. Manage Your Mindset

Many of us are quick to anger at the sight of squirrels scaring away birds, but it's helpful to see things from a different angle. "Framing it as a conflict or war is just going to escalate rather than address the problem," says John Griffin, director of urban wildlife at the Humane Society of the United States.

Instead, consider how their food caches help birds and plants. "Squirrels have an important role in our ecosystem and do a lot of things for us, like plant trees," John notes.

2. Narrow In on Behavior

Transplanting the squirrels with a safe-release trap is usually fatal for these furry creatures and won't prevent their friends from moving in. Instead, address their behaviors head-on in your yard.

3. Focus on Food

Consider adjusting your birdseed blend by incorporating food that squirrels tend to dislike, such as white millet, thistle and safflower seeds. Avoid allowing the seeds that are leftover or drop to build up on the ground; instead, give squirrels access to nuts and corn far from your feeders. Planting some native, natural food sources helps—sunflowers, fruit-producing plants and nut-bearing trees.

4. Explore Safe Solutions

There are plenty of squirrel-proof products available, so give some a try! Some feeders are responsive to a squirrel's weight and close the seed ports when they sense intruders. Add some baffles to your feeders or poles—or purchase a feeder that's battery-operated to spin the pesky critters off. Move feeders 10 feet away from the nearest jumping-off point, and hang them with thin metal cable or extra-strength fishing line.

Another option is attaching squirrel-spookers to poles. These movable plastic sleeves use a counterweight system to dump seed-snatchers to the ground.

Avoid greasing feeder poles, because it is harmful to birds and other wildlife. As a last resort, add capsaicin, a component found in chili peppers, to your seed. It leaves a bad taste in a squirrel's mouth, but birds don't mind it.

Inside the Nest

Take a peek into four of the most common types of bird homes.

Robin's nest and eggs

1. CUP Cup-shaped nests are the most common type found in backyards. Birds like American robins and blue jays build their cup nests on branches or ledges with twigs, grasses and sometimes manufactured materials such as string, cloth and paper.

An osprey perches on its platform nest.

2. PLATFORM Bald eagles and ospreys are among several species that construct their huge, somewhat flat, nests on platforms and in trees. The birds interweave large sticks, moss and grass to create these nests. One pair of bald eagles will reuse the same nest every year, so it can eventually weigh up to 2 tons.

A red-headed woodpecker pair near their nesting cavity.

Baltimore oriole hanging nest

3. HANGING Orioles like Bullock's, Baltimore and Altamira gather fibers, including twine and string, to create gourd-shaped pouches hanging from branches. The female oriole works on the nest from the inside and forms the bottom to the shape of her body.

STUFF WE LOVE

Read more about how birds build their nests in Into the Nest *by Laura Erickson and Marie Read.*

4. CAVITY Instead of creating a traditional nest, woodpecker species like downies and hairies carve out a nest cavity within a tree. Males and females take turns using their bills to dig and then line the bottom of the 6- to 15-inch-deep cavity with soft wood chips.

Flashy Feathers

Whether flickers are gobbling ants on the ground or climbing a tree trunk, their field marks get noticed.

Long, slightly downturned bill, ideal for foraging

Red mustache (only on red-shafted males)

Black chest patch

Tan belly with dark spots

Male red-shafted northern flicker

Gray-brown back with black bars

Wing feathers with red shafts

Pinkish red coloring on the underside of tail

Female yellow-shafted northern flicker

ONE SPECIES, TWO FORMS

A northern flicker is either red-shafted (in the West) or yellow-shafted (in the North and East). In the center of the continent, many flickers are intermediate between the two forms.

BIRDSEED

You might have birdseed, another common ingredient in suet, already on hand. Black oil sunflower, thistle and white millet seed are naturally high in fat or oils and give birds the energy to thrive in winter.

LARD

All good suet mixes need a solid base. Lard (pig fat) is a convenient replacement for traditional suet (the waxy fat around sheep and cow kidneys and loins). Most supermarket lard is already rendered and strained to remove any stray pieces of meat.

QUICK OATS

Ingredients like quick oats, cornmeal and flour help with the consistency of suet cakes. They make the mixture more crumbly and easier for birds to eat.

Make Your Own Suet

Add equal parts nutritious treats and creativity to mix up a combo your backyard birds will love.

PEANUTS

Super nutritious peanuts give birds a much-needed protein boost, plus they're high in fat. Be sure to use only unsalted, out of the shell peanuts in your blend.

RAISINS

Many birds eat fruit in the winter if it's readily available. Add raisins, cranberries, apples or chunks of dried fruit to your mix.

PEANUT BUTTER

Natural peanut butters are easy to melt, loaded with protein and fat, and can be used in combination with lard or beef fat as a base for your recipe. Try using crunchy peanut butter to add a nutty kick.

Red-Tailed *Traits*

Learn the key characteristics of these large hawks.

Sharp curved bill
to tear apart prey

Large deep eyes provide
excellent vision

The telltale
red tail color is
most noticeable
when an adult
red-tailed hawk
is in flight.

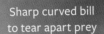

Stands almost
2 feet tall with a
4-foot wingspan

Dark brown
feathers on back,
face and wings,
plus a lighter belly
streaked with
brown feathers

Weighs less
than 3 pounds
despite a large,
bulky stature

THE BUTEO BUNCH

Red-tailed hawks, like this
one, are the most common
members of the buteo group.
These birds of prey are often
seen perched along roadsides
or soaring with barely a flap
of their wings. Raptors in the
buteo family have chunky
builds, broad wings and short
wide tails. Other members of
the buteo clan include broad-
winged, red-shouldered and
rough-legged hawks.

Four sharp talons
(one faces back) on
each foot capture
and hold prey

Feed Your Plants

Strong and healthy plants thrive with fertilizer. Here's how to give your garden a nutrient boost.

RECORD IT

Stay on top of your fertilizer applications by making notes on a calendar.

Shopping for fertilizer and applying it may seem perplexing at first. Follow these simple tips and you'll be fertilizing like a pro in no time.

READ THE LABEL

The front of every bag contains three numbers, such as 10-10-10 or 10-15-10 or 6-3-0. In order, these represent the percentage of nitrogen, phosphorus in the form of phosphate, and potassium in the form of potash. The rest of the material is filler that dilutes the fertilizer so it's easier to apply.

A nice balanced fertilizer (formulation 10-10-10 or 12-12-12) may seem suitable for most gardens, but this can lead to excessive levels of

SIGNS OF NUTRIENT DEFICIENCIES

NITROGEN
Pale green or yellowish lower leaves; slow growth.

POTASSIUM
Yellow or brown along older leaf edges. May have yellowing between veins, curling or spotting.

CALCIUM
Deformed or failed terminal buds and root tips. Results in blossom end rot in peppers and tomatoes.

PHOSPHORUS
A burned look on leaf tips; dark green or reddish purple older leaves.

SULFUR
Light green over the entire plant; yellowing of younger leaves.

IRON
Yellowing between veins of upper leaves leading to an eventual bleached look. Possibility of new leaves being yellowish white.

MANGANESE
Paling or yellowing of leaf tissue between veins, followed by spots that show on middle leaves first.

phosphorus and potassium, so it's important to conduct a soil test before choosing a fertilizer.

Many are also labeled as fast- or slow-release, indicating how quickly the nutrients become available to the plant. Fast-release types dissolve in water and are readily available. They are fast-acting and less expensive but pose a greater risk of fertilizer burn and groundwater pollution if misapplied. Slow-release types deliver small amounts of nutrients for plants to use over time. They have a lower burn potential and require fewer applications, but usually cost more.

HOW TO APPLY

Drop and broadcast spreaders apply granular fertilizer to large spaces, such as established grassy areas or unplanted large lawns, beds and gardens. In existing gardens, apply when the plants are dry. Brush off any granules that land on leaves. Lightly cultivate and then water, so the fertilizer soaks into the soil. Use hand-held spreaders for applying granular fertilizer to small or medium-size gardens. With this technique, fertilize only the plants that need it. Sprinkle on the ground around the base of plants and lightly scratch into the soil with a rake or trowel. Unless steady rain is predicted, water right away.

THE SPECIFICS

Annuals should be given a low-nitrogen formula. Use about 2 to 3 pounds per 100 square feet every season. Use a slow-release fertilizer one time, or make three 1-pound applications throughout the growing season. In areas with a long season, a midseason application may be needed.

Most ground covers need only one spring application of nitrogen-rich fertilizer, but those with flowers and fall color typically don't.

Perennials perform best when fertilized in spring with either compost or aged manure. Apply 2 inches every two to three years, using additional fertilizer as needed.

For potted plants, add a slow-release type to the soil mix before planting. Every time you water, a little fertilizer is released, providing a steady flow of nutrients. But depending on the growing conditions and number of plants in the container, a midseason boost may be needed.

Avoid overfertilizing trees and shrubs, which often get added nutrients from nearby fertilized plantings and lawns.

4 Weeds *to Know*

Either embrace or yank these misunderstood plants in your backyard.

BROAD-LEAVED PLANTAIN

To ease pain from a minor cut or sting, apply crushed broad-leaved plantain leaves to the wound for relief. The young leaves on this ground-hugging rosette also are high in calcium and vitamins. But if these plants are unwelcome garden guests, use a trowel to lift each one out of the ground, roots and all.

DANDELION

The seeds ripen just in time to nourish goldfinches and indigo buntings during their spring migration. Humans can enjoy dandelions, too! The greens go great in salads and taste similar to arugula. Use a forked-tip weeder to pop out the taproot.

PURPLE DEAD NETTLE

Unlike true nettle, dead nettle doesn't have painful, stinging hairs. This weed often blooms side by side with henbit, its similar-looking relative in the mint family. Yank out the plant in one big handful so that you don't have millions next year.

LAMBS' QUARTERS

Birds snack on its seeds all winter. It can also be used safely in small amounts in salads. But it aggressively self-sows, so bury seedlings with mulch and hand-pull taller plants if you want them gone.

THRILLERS
Tall plants with an upright growing habit

Place thriller Angelface Perfectly Pink summer snapdragon in the back for height.

FILLERS
Mounded-habit plants that fill space between the thriller and spiller

Insert filler Sweet Caroline Light Green sweet potato vine in front of the thriller.

SPILLERS
Plants with a trailing habit that spill over the sides of the pot

Add spiller Supertunia Picasso in Purple petunia closest to the pot's edge so blooms can flow over.

MAKE IT! This stunning container combo from Proven Winners was created in a 14-inch pot. It includes one summer snapdragon, two sweet potato vines and two petunias. When placed in full or part sun, the plants will thrive from summer into fall.

Use a potting mix that includes soil conditioners like vermiculite, peat moss and perlite.

Create the *Perfect Pot*

Follow the thriller, filler, spiller concept for easy-to-plant containers that pop.

CHAPTER 4

AMAZING
Hummingbirds

*Bird-watchers and gardeners everywhere are
delighted by these little sprites of nature.*

5 Secret *Hummingbird Hot Spots*

The West is best when it comes to hummingbirds. Variations in terrain and rainfall create diverse habitats that attract up to 17 species. At these must-visit parks, the odds are good you'll see many types of hummingbirds, including a few rare ones.

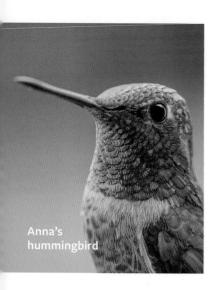

Anna's hummingbird

1 Desert National Wildlife Refuge

LAS VEGAS, NEVADA

While the Mojave Desert is certainly hot, it's also an extraordinary spot for hummingbirds. This 1.6-million-acre wildlife refuge, the largest outside of Alaska, attracts 320 species of birds, including many hummingbird species—more than any other birding destination in Nevada.

Watch for: Costa's hummingbirds, which thrive in arid climates, nest in the refuge during late winter and early spring. Black-chinned and Anna's hummingbirds also flit among the sagebrush and wetland habitats at the refuge.

Do it: Birders flock to the Corn Creek visitor center, where the vegetation attracts many migrant and vagrant hummingbirds. Several trails begin here, some accessible to all, for the best hummingbird-watching.

1.
DESERT NATIONAL WILDLIFE REFUGE
LAS VEGAS, NEVADA

2 Bandelier National Monument

LOS ALAMOS, NEW MEXICO

The Ancestral Pueblo people lived on the Pajarito Plateau in northern New Mexico until the mid-1500s, carving their homes into the volcanic tuff and farming atop the mesas in what is now Bandelier National Monument, a 33,000-acre park. It's a favorite destination among birders aiming to see not only many hummingbirds but a wide diversity of birds more typical of western mountains, canyons and grasslands.

Watch for: Broad-tailed and black-chinned hummingbirds raise families in Bandelier National Monument. Calliope and rufous hummingbirds flit among the monument's cliffs, valleys and streams.

Do it: While you are looking for the four hummingbird species found here, check the Bandelier Bird Checklist for other summer and migratory birds on your bucket list, like the hepatic tanager and Lazuli bunting.

3 Davis Mountains State Park

FORT DAVIS, TEXAS

Located in westernmost Texas, the Davis Mountains are hummingbird heaven from July to October. With both high elevation (5,000 feet) and levels of precipitation, the range is one of the Southwest's sky island environments, making it a mecca for birds and other wildlife. Most hummingbird species in the U.S. have been spotted here.

Watch for: Broad-tailed, black-chinned and rufous hummingbirds are common, but don't be surprised if lucifer, ruby-throated or Calliope hummers whiz by, too. Ornithologists found the first-ever amethyst-throated hummingbird in the U.S. here. Nearby McDonald Observatory and the Nature Conservancy's Davis Mountains Preserve maintain bird-viewing stations.

Do it: During the annual Davis Mountains Hummingbird Celebration, designated viewing spots in the park and in adjacent sanctuaries put you at the hummingbird hub, even on rainy days. Or join a workshop on how to garden for or properly feed these feisty sky-fairies.

2.
BANDELIER
NATIONAL
MONUMENT
LOS ALAMOS,
NEW MEXICO

Rufous
hummingbird

DAVIS MOUNTAINS
STATE PARK
FORT DAVIS, TEXAS

Violet-crowned hummingbird

4.
RAMSEY CANYON PRESERVE
HEREFORD, ARIZONA

4 Ramsey Canyon Preserve

HEREFORD, ARIZONA

The Huachuca Mountains, home to Ramsey Canyon Preserve, rise from the desert of southeastern Arizona and catch cooler air that creates both arid and subtropical microclimates in close proximity. As a result, the preserve is remarkably biodiverse, playing host to numerous hummingbird species.
Watch for: Ramsey Canyon attracts 15 species of hummingbirds, some of which migrate only this far north. It's a known hot spot for violet-crowned and berylline hummingbirds.

Do it: The Nature Conservancy offers guided walks from March through November in the Ramsey Canyon Preserve, with April through September being the best time for bird-watching.

5 Cabrillo National Monument

SAN DIEGO, CALIFORNIA

Cabrillo National Monument, a seaside preserve surrounded by urban sprawl, is an oasis for birds and other marine and terrestrial wildlife. The monument offers a chance to observe both resident and migratory hummingbird species.
Watch for: During mating season, male Anna's hummingbirds perform aerial acrobatics to attract a mate. Numerous coastal species winter here or migrate through, including Allen's, rufous, black-chinned and Costa's hummingbirds. In April, watch Calliope hummingbirds gather around the blooming bottlebrush trees.
Do it: Rangers offer guided tours and other activities daily. In addition to birding, they'll help you explore the tidal pools and watch for whales. Kids can pick up a Junior Ranger activity book at the visitor center to record the hummingbirds they see along the 2½-mile Bayside Trail and elsewhere in the park.

5.
CABRILLO NATIONAL MONUMENT
SAN DIEGO, CALIFORNIA

A Hummingbird *Home*

Zoom in on one of these teeny-tiny nests and take a tour of its artful structure.

The female smooths and shapes the inside of the nest using her body.

Lichens, mosses, plant down and fibers make up the nest and camouflage its exterior.

Her nest is big enough for two eggs, and incubation lasts 12 to 19 days.

She collects and weaves stretchy spider silk through the nest to hold it together, bind it to the supporting branch, and expand as the chicks grow.

Most nests are built in the fork of a tree or shrub, 10 to 40 feet above the ground.

A hummingbird nest is about the size of a quarter, and one egg is roughly the size of a jelly bean!

NO. 1 MOM

When it comes to the job of parenting, female hummingbirds do all the heavy lifting, from building the nest to raising the young. After both eggs hatch, the mother feeds her nestlings a slurry of nectar and keeps them warm. Once they're about 15 days old, she starts bringing them small insects, continuing to care for them until about a week after they leave the nest.

8 Flowers Hummingbirds *Love*

Readers captured energetic birds zipping through their gardens.
These nectar-rich blooms keep them buzzing back for more.

Ruby-throated at
bee balm by
William Friggle
DENVER, PENNSYLVANIA

Bee balm

Monarda, Zones 3 to 9

This plant definitely fits the bill. It's
vibrant, tube-shaped and full of nectar—
everything a hummingbird wants. Plant
bee balm in full sun and in well-draining
soil. Then sit back and enjoy the fragrant
flowers and the hummingbird show.

**Ruby-throated
at alstroemeria by
Maureen Szuniewicz**
DEPEW, NEW YORK

Alstroemeria

Alstroemeria, Zones 5 to 10

The vibrant, exotic look of this bulb is super attractive to hummingbirds. It's also a favorite of gardeners in the West.

Hosta

Hosta, Zones 3 to 8

Rising up to 3 feet above the foliage, hosta flowers are both nectar-filled and dainty. The blooms last up to six weeks, so they are always at the ready when a hummingbird stops by.

Ruby-throated at salvia by **Roslynn Long** BURNSVILLE, MINNESOTA

Salvia

Salvia, Zones 4 to 11

Salvia is a hummingbird favorite because many other nectar seekers, like bees and butterflies, are unable to access the nectar buried deep in the tubular blooms. That means more for hummingbirds!

Ruby-throated at hosta by **Mid Stutsman** GOSHEN, INDIANA

Ruby-throated at hibiscus by Tarek Aoun
CHARLOTTE, NORTH CAROLINA

Hibiscus

Hibiscus, Zones 4 to 9

This hardy favorite features flowers that span from 4 to 12 inches wide. It's a heat lover, so find a sunny spot and get ready to watch tiny birds visit the gigantic blooms.

Zinnia

Zinnia, Annual

For a quick pop of color in the summer garden, sun-loving zinnias are a must. Plant a combination of single-bloom varieties in red and bright pink if you want to make the yard more desirable to hummingbirds.

Ruby-throated at zinnia by **Michael Castelli**
HURLEY, NEW YORK

Crocosmia

Crocosmia, Zones 5 to 9

Fiery red-orange blossoms burst to life in mid- to late summer, offering your resident hummingbirds a sweet treat. For the best flowers, make sure to keep the soil moist.

Cape fuchsia

Phygelius, Zones 6 to 10

At 3 to 5 feet tall and wide, cape fuchsia commands attention in any garden, especially when the bright tube-shaped flowers are in bloom. A hummingbird's slender bill is a perfect fit!

Ruby-throated at crocosmia by Barbara Houlihan
MADISON, WISCONSIN

**Anna's at
cape fuchsia by
Roy Western**
OCEAN PARK,
WASHINGTON

BIRD BRAINS
Colorful rufous hummingbirds, like this male, have amazing memories. They often seek out and stop at the same feeders and flowers during their annual migration routes.

Toughest Bird on the Block

Get to know the feisty rufous hummingbird.

IF YOU RESIDE IN A NORTHWESTERN state, like Washington or Oregon, and you see a rumble break out at your backyard sugar-water feeder, a male rufous hummingbird is the likely culprit. Well-known for their aggressive nature, the rufous males are particularly antagonistic during the late-spring breeding season when territories are being established. Female rufous hummingbirds will also jump into the fray to protect their nesting territories and to drive off other rufous that get too close. They have even been known to chase chipmunks away.

Rufous are hard to miss as they zip, zoom and dive around sugar-water feeders. Male rufous hummingbirds have orange backs and bellies and iridescent red throats, while females and juveniles sport more subdued green coloring. The Allen's hummingbird, another species of the West, is often confused for the rufous. As a general rule of thumb, if the male's back is more orange than green, it's a rufous. Females and juveniles of both species are essentially identical.

During courtship, a male rufous dives in a J-shaped or steep oval pattern when a female enters his breeding territory. The male rufous doesn't stick with one female, though, and pairs up with multiple partners throughout a single breeding season.

That means the tough job of parenting falls entirely to the female rufous. She chooses a suitable nesting site and builds the small, cup-shaped nest herself using plant matter, such as lichen, moss and bark. She then lays two white jelly bean-sized eggs.

The mother feeds her two young until they leave the nest, about 21 days after hatching.

Female rufous

In western and southwestern states, it's easy to attract these feisty little birds with sugar-water feeders. Skip the red dye, though, and make your own sugar-water mixture by combining 1 part table sugar to 4 parts water.

To keep the peace at backyard feeders, set up more than one and place each feeder at a distance and out of sight of the others. If multiple feeders are available, an aggressive rufous hummingbird is more willing to share.

Another option is to plant a few nectar-rich red blooms, such as bee balm and penstemon. Tube-shaped blooms also work well.

Even if you're outside their range, a rufous may still visit your yard. Of all western hummingbird species, the rufous is most likely to wander. In their southward migration in late summer and fall, rufous spread out across the western half of the continent, and some stray farther. They've been spotted in fall in every eastern state, and dozens spend the winter along the Gulf Coast.

Nectar *Perfection*

These easy-to-grow annuals are filled with the sweet stuff hummingbirds and butterflies can't resist.

1

WINGED WONDER
For maximum butterfly and hummingbird traffic in your garden, choose plants that bloom at various times from May through frost.

1 Salvia
SALVIA

Also commonly known as firecracker plant, this annual variety of salvia pops in any sunny garden, producing season-long color. Depending on the cultivar, this annual reaches 8 inches to 2 feet, though newer varieties are on the compact side.

Why we love it:
Tons of nectar-rich tubular blooms cover the short or long stalks. Flowers may be red, orange, white, blue, pink or purple.

2 Impatiens
IMPATIENS

Invite winged creatures into your shady spaces with impatiens, which come in a rainbow of hues. Once planted, they don't need much care. Even deadheading isn't necessary! Avoid downy mildew with disease-resistant SunPatiens and New Guinea impatiens.

Why we love it:
Reaching 6 inches to 2 feet high, it forms mounds, making it a good choice for borders and foundation beds, as well as for containers.

3 Fuchsia
FUCHSIA

These showy, pendulous blooms in red, white, pink and purple will capture your heart. There are more than 100 kinds, from low-growing dwarfs and trailing plants to upright shrubs. Fertilize weekly for best results.

Why we love it: Fuchsia grows best in moist soil and partial shade, so it's ideal for attracting hummingbirds to less-than-sunny yards.

4 Calibrachoa
CALIBRACHOA

Small petunialike flowers steal the show all season, making fast-growing calibrachoa a hot choice for beds and containers—especially those

that are geared toward hummingbirds and butterflies. Use it as a nicely textured filler plant or as a bold stand-alone. Plants reach about 8 inches tall and spread out.

Why we love it: It'll trail up to 16 inches before you know it, so use it as a fast-grower to quickly dress up a pot.

5 Cleome

CLEOME HASSLERIANA

Plant this tropical native in your garden and you're sure to attract the attention of your favorite fliers. This bloom, which some call spider flower, is a top nectar source for swallowtail butterflies and hummingbirds.

Why we love it: Cleome's tall stems topped by wispy pink, purple or white flowers are hard to miss. Plants tend to reseed themselves from one year to the next—if goldfinches don't get to them first.

6 Flowering tobacco

NICOTIANA

For a no-fuss way to liven up your garden, plant flowering tobacco. Ranging from 10 inches to 5 feet high, the stems are covered with star-shaped flowers in shades of red, maroon, lavender, white, pink, yellow and even green.

Why we love it: Some types, like *N. sylvestris* species, have a lovely scent in the evening. Grow it near a patio or entry so you can enjoy the fragrance.

7 Mexican sunflower

TITHONIA ROTUNDIFOLIA

This fast-growing annual, which blooms in late summer and autumn, reaches 6 feet in height. Its long-lasting orange and red flowers glow in full sun. Resist the urge to deadhead them—backyard songbirds enjoy the seeds.

Why we love it: It's a great pollinator magnet! Bumblebees, honeybees, swallowtails, fritillaries, skippers and more will stop by for a nectar snack.

8 Nasturtium

TROPAEOLUM

Humans aren't the only ones who enjoy nasturtiums: Moth and butterfly caterpillars like to munch on the leaves, as do some songbirds. The nectar attracts many types of fliers. Once it's established, nasturtium contributes vivid color all season long. It's easy to care for with regular watering. Some types grow in mounds, while others are good climbers.

Why we love it: The flower also makes a zesty, colorful addition to a green salad.

9 Lantana

LANTANA CAMARA

With profuse tiny flowers, there's plenty of nectar for both hummingbirds and butterflies. Smaller varieties with a mounding or trailing habit work

well in containers. If you live in a tropical climate or Zones 8 to 11, try lantana as a shrub or a perennial.

Why we love it: Songbirds nibble on black berries later in the growing season.

10 Zinnia
ZINNIA

Nectar-filled zinnias come in a broad range of colors, heights and flower sizes, and they are a cheerful addition to any backyard. Incredibly simple to start from seed, sun-loving zinnias bloom quickly. Seek out mildew-resistant varieties if mildew disease is a problem in your area.

Why we love it: A hummingbird and butterfly favorite, this versatile plant also has seed heads that attract sparrows, finches and juncos.

Flying Gems

Hummingbirds zip and zoom at high speeds through backyards, but these readers were lucky enough to capture the magic on camera.

This black-chinned hummingbird family of three settled into a tree near our house two years ago. The nest was the size of a small espresso cup and the eggs looked like white jelly beans. I felt so fortunate to be able to photograph the babies as they matured and fledged.

Melissa Cheatwood BERTRAM, TEXAS

The hummingbirds were zipping around the sugar-water feeders, so I patiently sat on my front porch with my camera at the ready. I took a lot of pictures before finally getting this one. This particular male ruby-throat was very protective of "his" feeder and was trying to scare off all the others.

Elisabeth Kelley MILLBROOK, ALABAMA

SAY CHEESE!

Patience is key for a good hummingbird photo. Over a few hours, gradually set up your tripod and camera so the birds get used to them. Use a wireless remote control to take photos and keep your subjects comfortable.

I snapped this photo of an Anna's hummingbird last year on Valentine's Day. It was enjoying the much-needed rain after some hot, dry Arizona weather. I like how its torso is shaped like a heart in this image.

Lisa Swanson
MARICOPA, ARIZONA

One rainy afternoon in June, a female ruby-throat took a little break from buzzing around the flowers and feeders to perch on the hummingbird swing. She stayed there for some time, and it was fun to grab the camera and capture the moment. I love how fluffed and ruffled her feathers are from the rain.

Lauren Slack WATERVILLE, MAINE

SWING TIME!

Hang perches, like a hummingbird swing, near sugar-water feeders for hummingbirds to rest on.

This young male Anna's perfectly exudes the stunning beauty of all hummingbirds. He is busy, yet peaceful, as he sips nectar from purple sage.

Paula Fleitell
EUGENE, OREGON

Here in Las Vegas, we have the pleasure of seeing and hosting hummingbirds all year long. This beautiful male Costa's frequently visits my backyard, and I was lucky enough to snap his photo.
Mark Rasmussen LAS VEGAS, NEVADA

I gave two of my grandsons cameras for Christmas. During a visit earlier this year, my husband and I took them on a bird walk through San Elijo Lagoon in Cardiff, California. Our cameras clicked away when we saw ducks and egrets, and the excitement was especially high for our fledgling photographers, ages 7 and 4. Imagine the joy when this beautiful male Costa's perched in front of us. His brilliant plumage caught the light perfectly.
Marilyn Barnes
COBLESKILL, NEW YORK

PHOTOS
of the
YEAR

Enjoy these gorgeous shots from the past year of *Birds & Blooms* magazine. Go to *birdsandblooms.com/ submit* to contribute.

1 Calliope hummingbird
Elijah Gildea
REDDING, CALIFORNIA

2 Anna's hummingbird
Lisa Swanson
MARICOPA, ARIZONA

3 Rufous hummingbird
Renae Tolbert
REDDING, CALIFORNIA

CHAPTER 5

BIRD *Tales*

What better way to navigate the seasons than with colorful birds captured here by readers.

Spring

Cardinals, some of my all-time favorites, visit my yard every day year-round. During the spring, they often perch in my blooming crabapple tree. I love this time of year when birds sing and blooms show their beauty.

Rebecca Granger
BANCROFT, MICHIGAN

I captured this American redstart

during a stroll in Hammonasset Beach State Park in Madison, Connecticut. To get the best light possible, I take walks in early morning and try to position myself in a spot where the quality, character and direction of light are in my favor. Then I wait quietly for birds to enter the good light. I use bird photography as a form of meditation, so being patient is actually the easy part.

William Canosa
BRANFORD, CONNECTICUT

In the past, I had only a couple of oriole visitors for a short time. But last year I put out plenty of oranges and grape jelly, and I saw up to six orioles each day at my feeder. They sure do like the oranges!

Diana Wolfe
MACY, INDIANA

Last year was the first time a pair of tree swallows chose to nest in one of our handmade boxes. We watched as both parents worked together to build the nest and gather food for their three babies. The adults took turns keeping guard on top of the box and hunting for insects. They didn't seem bothered by our presence and allowed us to get close while we weeded our nearby flower bed. Nature is beautiful, and this photo is a reminder for us all.

Tammy Hileman CELINA, OHIO

In just seven hours, a robin built a nest in the pansy planter on my doorstep. Soon after, I noticed she had laid a single blue egg.
Carol Keskitalo
NEW YORK MILLS, MINNESOTA

This common yellowthroat looked anything but common while it sang in a field of purple lupine in Rangeley, Maine. I especially like the glowing contrast of the bright yellow warbler with the rich violet of the flowers.
Christopher Ciccone
WOBURN, MASSACHUSETTS

Summer

**Summer
is very short**
in Manitoba, but this
photo definitely helps
relieve the harshness
of winter. It exudes the
true excitement and
color of summer.
Sujata Basu
WINNIPEG, MANITOBA

My husband spoke to me

in a soft, hurried voice: "Honey, don't move." I froze. I looked at him and saw him point up. I raised my eyes and saw a yellow-throated warbler. It was hard to contain my excitement as that tiny, gorgeous bird sat on our antique triangle dinner bell. Once it flew away, my husband urged me to add it to our farm list—it was No. 61. The warbler came back for several days, and we watched it munch on sunflower chips at our feeder (shown here) and gather horse hair. We hope to see this species around here again.

Robin Seeber
WEST ALEXANDER,
PENNSYLVANIA

A male California quail

hopped onto a boulder in our backyard to get a better view. He was surrounded by wild California poppies (our state flower). I grabbed my Canon EOS 7D camera with 100-400mm lens and captured this moment. I enjoy nature photography and keep my camera ready for the unexpected, even in my backyard.

Philip Robertson
LINCOLN, CALIFORNIA

Although bald eagles aren't typical backyard birds, here on the eastern shore of Virginia they're a common sight. I've seen many eagles over the past few years, and I'm still amazed at how majestic and graceful they are. It's only appropriate that the eagle is our country's national bird.

Lisa Gurney
ONANCOCK, VIRGINIA

While hunting for sunflower fields, I was surprised to see a small group of burrowing owls. This one was sitting on top of a roadside shrub, ready for its close-up. The owls weren't skittish at all as I lifted my camera to snap a photo.

Carol Nelson
GEORGETOWN, CALIFORNIA

I was lucky to spot this cedar waxwing gulping down as many of these tiny crabapples as it could get. I love the brilliant color accents of these birds and how they chat to each other while tossing back berries by the dozens. They're amazing to watch.

Kat Durant
SMITHS FALLS, ONTARIO

Blue grosbeaks are a breathtaking sight. One morning, I captured this male scanning his surroundings along an overgrown section of brush. It was on the edge of a salt marsh, and I saw dozens of other grosbeaks, too. I felt blessed to see such a strikingly beautiful bird.

Rick Hamilton
WESTMINSTER, MARYLAND

These two blue jays

were just starting an aerial courtship chase when I captured this photo. I've been studying jays for a few years. There is so much to observe, especially when it comes to their group dynamics.

Isabelle Marozzo
NORLAND, ONTARIO

The common loon

is Minnesota's state bird. I've lived here all my life and I had never seen one until I visited my dad's lake cabin north of the cities. One of his neighbors offered to take me out on the lake to look for its resident loon. We eventually found it on the lake's far side. The sun was starting to set, and the light reflected beautifully on the water.

Justin Pruden
ST. PAUL, MINNESOTA

Gulls have a bad reputation,
but I think they look elegant and striking in
this picture. They are one of my favorite birds,
and I love their silly antics. These laughing gulls
were hunting for food and chasing each other.
Steve Farmer KENNESAW, GEORGIA

This male ruby-throated

hummingbird landed
on a branch with
an American flag in
the background. It's
a perfect photo for
the Fourth of July!

Joey Herron
FAIRMONT,
WEST VIRGINIA

Autumn

The sun was setting as this female northern cardinal perched on a branch, waiting for her turn at the feeder. The warm light from the sun hitting her feathers made her look all the more beautiful and eye-catching.

Carolyn Stuart KANNAPOLIS, NORTH CAROLINA

Although it's a common species in the East, the tufted titmouse's range doesn't extend far into my state. So I was thrilled when I saw this one coming and going between my feeders and the nearby woods. I'm so glad I captured it and the background fall colors in this photo.
Patty Jennings
STACYVILLE, MAINE

My backyard is one of my favorite places to watch nature. I was keeping an eye out for visiting deer when I saw movement in the trees. This stunning barred owl caught my attention and looked as if it was posing for its portrait.
Wanda Donihoo
JULIETTE, GEORGIA

It's the loud squawking

from above that lets me know sandhill cranes have arrived in Albuquerque each fall. I captured these two slowly strolling through the grass just seconds before they took flight.

Karen Jones
RIO RANCHO,
NEW MEXICO

I often watched geese

and mallards at nearby Evergreen Lake, but I'd never heard of a wood duck before. So when a friend mentioned seeing some wood ducks at Sterne Park in Littleton, I was curious. We came upon the colorful birds swimming in the park's pond. What a lovely fall afternoon it was!

Ann Zimmerman
IDAHO SPRINGS,
COLORADO

I was in the process of building a deck that overlooks this fountain when a Cooper's hawk flew in. When I saw it, I texted my wife and asked her to bring my camera outside, and to be very careful as she opened the sliding door. I was about 60 feet away from the hawk and noticed that it seemed to be mesmerized by its reflection in the water bubble.

Stephen Smith AURORA, COLORADO

Winter

I waited all winter for this noble varied thrush to come close enough for a portrait. The bird skirted the edge of my property, just outside of camera range, searching for food. It wasn't until a rare snowfall covered its feeding grounds that it came to see what I was serving at my feeders.

Sally Harris
CARLSBORG,
WASHINGTON

On a cold, gloomy winter

day, I was driving through a particularly boggy area in Minnesota, hoping I would see something to photograph. Before I knew it, I came across this majestic great gray owl. It stared me down as I snapped this amazing shot.

Paul Danaher
CHICAGO HEIGHTS, ILLINOIS

Brilliantly colored blue

jays are some of my favorite winter birds. This particular one looks like it's trying to show off and say, "I'm going to pretend I don't see you taking my picture, but here is my good side."

Noelle Sippel
WEBSTER, NEW YORK

This is one of my favorite photographs of a yellow-rumped warbler. It was winter and there were no leaves on my trees. The bird hopped from branch to branch, posing for me before it flew away.

Betsy Moseley
ZELLWOOD, FLORIDA

We love feeding and watching

birds year-round at our home. Each winter, we are lucky to have the most colorful flickers show up to gobble down the suet.

Karen Osadchey
RIGBY, IDAHO

I see dark-eyed juncos almost daily in my backyard. Although I know they can be found on much of the continent, it seems as if they are all right here in North Carolina! The juncos mostly feed on the ground, but occasionally they fly to the feeders or use my little birdbath. I think they are just so adorable.

Kimberly Miskiewicz
RALEIGH,
NORTH CAROLINA

CHAPTER 6

Blooming
BEAUTIES

Please your senses with these fragrant flowers and eye-catching plants.

Perennials With *Staying Power*

Move over annuals! These hardworking plants pop up every year, put on a season-long flower show and save you money in the long run.

ANNUALS ARE LIKELY your go-to's for a long season of flowers, but some perennials give them a run for their money. Long-blooming types are tough, dependable and flower for six weeks or more. That's a bonus for pollinators, because they'll have a source of food every year. Perhaps best of all, buying perennials means you only pull out your wallet once, then sit back and reap the rewards of money well-spent.

"Any long-blooming perennials are a worthwhile investment," says Justin Hancock, horticulturist at Costa Farms, one of the largest growers in North America. "They give you tons of blooms over the course of months and come back every year, so every season, the display is better than the year before. Who doesn't love the idea of planting something once that blooms constantly and comes back every year?"

At the garden center this spring, reach for these tough, long-blooming perennials.

Pinch off spent coneflower blooms on a regular basis to make them last throughout the summer months.

Rose campion's pretty pink blooms

Coneflower

This beauty is a common grower in prairie plantings everywhere and for good reason: It succeeds in a wide range of conditions. A dependable performer in the intense heat of summer, it never fails to please with its large, colorful flowers. Growing 2 to 5 feet tall, coneflower traditionally offers purplish pink petals surrounding golden disks, but newer cultivars are white, yellow, orange, tomato red and pink. Zones 3 to 8.

Shasta daisy

Becky is a common cultivar with a classic look that will put a smile on your face. Divide Shasta daisies every three years to invigorate the blooms and encourage longevity. The large 3- to 4-inch-wide flowers bloom from midsummer into fall if deadheaded. These sturdy, upright plants grow 1 to 3 feet tall, so they won't overpower your garden. Zones 4 to 9.

Rose campion

Also known as mullein pink and dusty miller, rose campion is a short-lived perennial that never seems to disappear. Because it self-seeds freely, young plants are always ready to take over. Plants reach 2 to 3 feet, with bright magenta flowers that rise above velvety gray foliage. Some cultivars have white or red flowers, or white blooms with pink centers. Drought tolerant. Zones 4 to 8.

Butterfly Blue
pincushion flower

Long-blooming
Rocketman Russian
sage has strong stems
that prevent it from
flopping over.

Russian sage

Gardeners grow this popular perennial for
many reasons: It's deer resistant; it tolerates
heat, wind, drought and poor soil; and pollinators
love it. Plus it blooms for a good, long time. The
purplish blue flowers appear from midsummer
to early fall, complementing the aromatic gray-
green foliage. Russian sage grows 3 to 5 feet
tall and features a relaxed, open habit. To avoid
having to stake, place Russian sage in back of
a sturdy companion to keep it upright. Or choose
a dwarf form that matures at about $2^1/_2$ feet.
Zones 4 to 9.

Pincushion flower

The Butterfly Blue pincushion flower deserves
a starring role in more gardens. For starters, its
lavender-blue flowers are butterfly magnets. The
unique blooms, which rise up on 12- to 15-inch
wiry stems, look like miniature pincushions and
produce blooms from spring to frost. Because of its
small size and long bloom period, Butterfly Blue is
well-suited for the front of borders. Zones 3 to 7.

Daisy May
Shasta daisy

Moonbeam coreopsis

For continuous blooms, try Strawberry Seduction yarrow.

Coreopsis

Moonbeam coreopsis is worthy of a spot in your garden just for its airy green foliage. But in summer, it's topped by a profusion of creamy yellow flowers, providing all the more reason to plant it. Shear the spent flowers to get extra blooms in fall. Moonbeam grows 12 to 18 inches tall and makes a nice front-of-border plant. It's not only tolerant of heat and humidity; it does well in dry, rocky soils. Zones 3 to 9.

Yarrow

Strawberry Seduction yarrow is a beauty, thanks to clusters of dusty red flowers with yellow centers that appear throughout the summer. The flowers are small but numerous, rising 18 to 24 inches; they fade to hues of light pink and brown. It tends to spread, so divide every few years to contain it. Zones 3 to 9.

Black-eyed Susan

Most black-eyed Susans are well-known for having a long bloom period, but Little Goldstar takes it up one notch. Its bright golden yellow flowers with chocolate centers appear from midsummer to early fall. These butterfly favorites grow 2 to 3 feet tall and are sturdy enough to stand without staking. They'll adapt to dry and moist soils and even heavy clay, but they do best in a well-draining soil with ample moisture. Little Goldstar looks great in a border or a container. Deer resistant. Zones 4 to 8.

Sedum

Sedum (not pictured) is a lazy gardener's best friend: Plant it and forget it. Popular cultivars such as Autumn Joy grow only 18 to 24 inches tall and feature attractive blue-green succulent leaves that resist animal browsing. Grow sedum in well-draining soil and full sun for best results. This mounded perennial looks great in late summer and early fall, when flowers mature to pink or rusty red, depending on the cultivar. The flowers are attractive even after they turn brown, so leave them for winter interest. Zones 3 to 8.

Veronica

Sunny Border Blue veronica produces a dense clump of crinkled green foliage topped by violet-blue flower spikes from summer to fall if deadheaded. Sunny Border Blue grows 18 to 24 inches tall. A pollinator favorite, this veronica also makes a perfect cut flower. It is adaptable to different soils as long as they drain well. Zones 4 to 8.

MAXIMIZE THE BLOOM POTENTIAL

Use these tips to get the most from your long-blooming perennials.

Keep up with deadheading. "By removing faded flowers, you give the plants the opportunity to recycle energy into producing more flowers rather than seeds," says Justin Hancock, horticulturist at Costa Farms. The only exception: Leave late-season flowers in place for winter interest and to feed wildlife.

Plant your perennials in the right spot. When a perennial gets the right light and moisture, it produces more, and often bigger, flowers. Good soil prep helps, too. If you have poor soil, adding lots of composted organic matter before planting can make a huge difference.

Include perennials with a range of overlapping bloom times. Intermix some self-seeding annuals, such as larkspur in spring and cleome in summer and fall, to really stretch the show.

Black-eyed Susan

Watch butterflies devour the nectar inside Sunny Border Blue veronica's flowers. The blooms last for more than four weeks!

Oriental
poppies

Poppies *Aplenty*

Fall is the best time to plant these classic beauties for jaw-dropping summer color.

Prickly poppy

A SUMMER GARDEN FILLED with colorful poppies starts in autumn!

Either let your poppies dry out and naturally scatter seeds at the end of the growing season or sprinkle a packet of seeds over bare soil in a sunny spot. Whichever way you get the seeds to the soil, they require light to germinate, so ignore the urge to tuck them in.

Fall-sown seeds germinate when the time is right. Some sprout in fall and overwinter, even in cold climates. Those seedlings usually become the biggest, most vigorous plants—and they bloom the earliest. Other fall-sown seeds wait until early spring to emerge.

If you miss fall planting time, scatter poppy seeds whenever there's no snow on the ground during winter through very early spring. The cold-tolerant seedlings germinate weeks before cosmos, zinnias and other self-sowing annuals.

California poppy

Transplanting with Taproots

During fall and at the seedling stage is the best time to transplant. Because all poppies have taproots, moving plants, even very young seedlings, is tricky—though still possible. "I've transplanted many poppies!" says Jennifer Bouseelot, an Iowa native who teaches horticulture at Colorado State University.

Unlike plants with fibrous roots, a tap-rooted plant is unable to quickly grow new roots to make up for damage. "Taproots don't like to be disturbed," Jennifer says. Be sure to dig deep and keep the soil as intact as possible.

To transplant a poppy, including a seedling, dig deep to lift the plant out of its current space, being careful to keep the soil in one piece around the roots. Slide it gently into a new hole, firm it in and keep it moist until the plant settles.

When to Divide Oriental Poppies

If you've ever wondered why the big seedpods of your glorious Oriental clump never seem to sow any seeds, it's because most of the plants sold today are complex hybrids. Crossbred from three original species (*Papaver orientale*, *P. pseudo-orientale* and *P. bracteatum*), most, if not all, of the seeds in those pods are sterile.

Oriental poppies

Flanders poppies add major impact when grown in large groups.

You can still multiply that clump by making a division in fall. And if the spot where the plant is growing is a lackluster spot, move the whole thing. The secret is to work with the plant's natural cycle.

Oriental poppies die and disappear in summer, a survival trick from their original Persian homelands (in what is now Iran), where the mountains are hot and dry in summer. In fall, new growth appears, and that's the signal it's time to dig. The autumn urge to grow helps poppies settle in quickly, and the roots won't have to support fully grown foliage and flowers.

Pick the Perfect Poppy

Poppies may seem fragile, but they're hardy characters, shrugging off cold winters and dry summers. Even the big, lush Orientals flourish in dry areas. "The poppies I grow get almost no irrigation," Jennifer says. "They only receive the 15 inches of annual rainfall that we get along the front range of Colorado. But they thrive!"

Growing from seed is always the best way to experience the charms of annual poppies or to expand your collection of cheerful, citrus-colored biennial Iceland poppies (*Papaver nudicaule*), a sure sign of spring at garden centers. "Iceland poppy is kind to me," Jennifer says. "It germinates well." Sow the seed in fall—like all seed-grown poppies, it does best in cool weather.

Shirley poppies feature thin, delicate petals.

Prune yellow Iceland poppies for a second round of blooms in fall.

THE PASS-ALONG POPPY MYSTERY

If you spot a big, dense bed of fluffy orange-red Oriental-like poppies blooming near an old house, you've discovered a heritage perennial of forgotten name and origin. The plant looks a lot like a double Oriental, but instead of staying in a clump, this antique poppy spreads quickly by underground stems called stolons that root as they go.

This perennial rarely shows up on the market. If you want to try growing it and spot a big bed in bloom, make the acquaintance of the gardener. They might share with you! Come back in fall and dig deep to get a start for your own yard.

Shirley poppy blooms shine among fresh buds and seed pods.

For on-trend color, sow gleaming orange California poppies (*Eschscholzia californica*) in fall. Creamy white, rosy purple, glowing red-orange and frilly double-flowered versions are lovely alongside the classic orange. Plant burgundy celosia behind them in spring for a stylish splash.

Bright red Flanders (*Papaver rhoeas*), also known as field or corn poppies, are grown for their spectacular color. This fiery bloom is splashed across Van Gogh's paintings. It later became the inspiration for Poppy Day, with paper poppies distributed in memory of the fallen soldiers of World War I and the pretty wildflowers that sprouted profusely in the disturbed ground.

In your garden, try sowing some Flanders poppies among ornamental grasses, next to silvery gray plants or along a white fence for maximum impact.

Embrace the unexpected with delicate Shirley poppies (*Papaver rhoeas*). This two-toned bloom originated in the late 1800s in Shirley, England, when a vicar spotted an oddball among thousands of poppies. Instead of being all red, its petals had white edges. From the seeds of that mutant, he developed the Shirley strain, a mix of pinks, salmons and whites with contrasting edges. Single colors are available, but the old-time mix is the most fun. You never know what color the blooms will be until the plump buds pop!

Keep an eye on seed books and garden centers for different poppy varieties, such as the snowy white crested prickly poppy (*Argemone polyanthemos*). Jennifer says, "The blousy white flowers are a visual treat during the dry, hot summers of the West."

Monarch on milkweed

Milkweed *Matters*

This plant is critical to the survival of monarch butterflies.

6
If it's possible, start your milkweed seeds indoors under artificial lights. The seedlings will be ready to transplant in the garden once they are 3 to 6 inches tall and when the threat of frost has passed. Plan for about four to eight weeks of indoor growing time.

3
A milkweed native to your specific area is the best option, but these three can be planted almost anywhere: common, swamp and butterfly weed.

65
While the tropical milkweed plant (*Asclepias curassavica*) is nonnative, it's beneficial to monarchs. But it doesn't die back in the southern U.S. and California, leaving monarchs susceptible to a parasite. Cut back tropical milkweed for the cool months— or replace it with one of the more than 65 native varieties out there.

4
After the dainty milkweed flowers stop blooming, their 2- to 4-inch seedpods burst open to reveal silky seeds that fly away with the wind.

90
The population of monarch butterflies has declined by as much as 90 percent in the last 20 years. Loss of habitat, milkweed and other native nectar plants is a major reason.

1
Milkweed is the one plant monarch butterflies rely on to successfully complete their life cycles. Adult females lay eggs only on milkweed leaves.

Rain Garden
Favorites

Water-loving plants make a splash among birds, butterflies and bugs.
These natives put spring showers to good use!

1

1 Blue cardinal flower

LOBELIA SIPHILITICA, ZONES 4 TO 9

Spires of beautiful blue flowers appear in mid- to late summer. It blooms later and tends to live longer than the red cardinal flower, a relative. Give this sun-loving perennial a bit of shade if your summers are very hot, and plant it in the wettest part of your rain garden.

Why we love it: It attracts native bees, bumblebees, birds and hummingbirds. Plus it's deer-resistant!

2 Buttonbush

CEPHALANTHUS OCCIDENTALIS, ZONES 4 TO 9

Add fragrance and seasonal beauty to sunny rain gardens with this native shrub. Butterflies, hummingbirds and bees are sure to stop by the aromatic flowers in early summer. Later, round fruits replace the flowers and persist into winter.

Why we love it: With new compact varieties, such as upright Ping Pong at 6 feet tall and Sugar Shack at only 3 to 4 feet tall, buttonbush is suitable for most landscapes.

3 Blue-eyed grass

SISYRINCHIUM ANGUSTIFOLIUM, ZONES 4 TO 9

You may be surprised to learn that this grasslike grower is actually a member of the iris family. Violet-blue flowers appear in spring. Grow blue-eyed grass in full sun to partial shade and moist to wet soil for best results. This is a perfect plant for areas that tend to stay moist.

Why we love it: Bring the blooms indoors—it makes a terrific cut flower for a spring bouquet.

4 Turtlehead

CHELONE GLABRA, ZONES 3 TO 8

Finish off summer and segue into fall with unique flowers shaped like turtle heads. Spikes of pink-tinged white flowers top 2- to 3-foot-tall plants. Add a spot of color with Hot Lips, a variety with bright pink flowers and red stems.

Why we love it: It's a host plant for the Baltimore checkerspot butterfly caterpillar, and the flowers attract many pollinators.

5 Firedance dogwood

CORNUS SERICEA 'FIREDANCE', ZONES 2 TO 7

This four-season beauty adds to any rain garden's year-round charm. White spring blossoms turn into white berries that attract birds. The show continues into fall as leaves turn red-purple and eventually drop to reveal brilliant red stems.

Why we love it: This compact red twig dogwood packs a lot of beauty into its 3- to 4-foot-tall size.

6 Palm branch sedge

CAREX MUSKINGUMENSIS, ZONES 4 TO 9

It's all about the foliage with this one. The glossy leaves glisten in the sun and pair well with other plants. When conditions are right, it creates a nice ground cover that weaves through nearby plants.

Why we love it: Palm sedge tolerates partial shade and full sun. It supports pollinators and butterflies, and birds feed on its seeds. Plus it's resistant to deer.

7 Chokeberry

ARONIA SPECIES, ZONES 3 TO 9

This suckering native shrub has it all—spring flowers, glossy green leaves, vibrant red fall color and winter fruit. The antioxidant-rich berries will make you pucker; even the birds leave them be until mid- to late winter, when other food sources are scarce.

Why we love it: Newly introduced Low Scape Hedger and Low Scape Mound offer shorter, narrower options to expand design possibilities.

8 Swamp milkweed

ASCLEPIAS INCARNATA, ZONES 3 TO 6

Native to swamps and wet meadows, this butterfly and hummingbird magnet also tolerates dry soil. The 3- to 4-foot-tall plants are topped with fragrant showy pink to mauve flowers in mid- to late summer.

Why we love it: You'll find both monarch and queen butterfly caterpillars munching on the leaves, while deer tend to leave it be.

9 Swamp rose mallow

HIBISCUS MOSCHEUTOS, ZONES 4 TO 9

Flowers the size of dinner plates are sure to make visitors and passers-by stop for a second look. It may start off a little slow in spring, but the showstopper could reach 3 to 7 feet tall. Mark its location to avoid accidentally weeding out this late-sprouting perennial.

Why we love it: The impressive 8-inch blooms can be white, pink or crimson.

10 Winterberry

ILEX VERTICILLATA, ZONES 3 TO 9

Light up your fall and winter rain garden with this deciduous holly. The bright red berries take center stage as the leaves drop in fall. For fruit to set, you'll need at least one male for up to five female plants.

Why we love it: Berry-laden stems combine nicely with evergreens to create an outdoor winter container—away from pets and children.

White
Casablanca
lily

The *Blooms & the Bees*

Take a deep dive into how flower pollination works. There's a lot more to it than meets the eye!

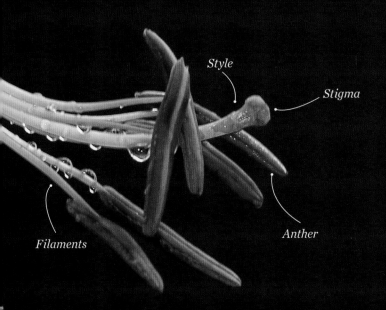

Style

Stigma

Anther

Filaments

ANATOMY OF A FLOWER

Anther: male part of the flower that produces pollen.

Filaments: stalks that support the anthers.

Stigma: base for pollen.

Style: female part of the flower that connects stigma to flower.

Stamen: the sum of anther and filament.

IN NATURE, THE QUEST TO SURVIVE and spread is essential. And that's certainly true for flowers. We might see them as vibrant harbingers of spring or precursors to juicy tomatoes, but from the flower's perspective, it's just trying to live and reproduce.

"Flowers are basically brightly colored, sweet-smelling adverts announcing that they have nectar and pollen," says Matthew Shepherd of the Xerces Society for Invertebrate Conservation. "It's the botanical equivalent of a neon breakfast sign in a diner window."

The Basics

Pollination is the transfer of pollen from a plant's male parts, the stamens, to the female parts, or pistils, a pairing that creates seeds. "More than 80 percent of flowering plants rely on a bee or other pollinator for this to happen," Matthew says.

The pistil's most visible part is a single central stalk called the style; the sticky head on top is the stigma. The style leads to the ovary within the flower, which contains ovules that will become seeds once fertilized.

And the showy parts of the stamen are the anthers, where pollen is made and stored. Typically, they rise above the flower on stems called filaments.

But the shape, size and number of female pistils and male stamens varies widely by flower type. For example, an Asiatic lily has a single style that rises above six flashy, pollen-filled anthers. But on a hibiscus, a central style is covered with dozens of stamens, short filaments topped with anthers that look like mini mushroom caps. With some other flowers, you have to look closely to see any distinct parts.

The Details

To the human eye, pollen grains look like powder, but the yellow or orange smudge they leave on your finger contains thousands of microscopic vessels of genetic information protected by hard outer shells and an oily coating, which keeps them together on the anther or in transport.

Pollination takes place when pollen lands on a stigma, germinates and grows a tube down through the style into the ovary. There, male

THE POWER OF FLOWERS

To attract more pollinators, grow a diverse variety of plants native to your area. Here are five to try.

1 BEE BALM
This summer favorite easily attracts bees, butterflies and hummingbirds.

2 MILKWEED
It's not just for monarchs! Many varieties of this perennial offer attractive nectar sources.

3 CATMINT
With long-lived blooms, catmint entices plenty of pollinators and is deer-resistant.

4 SEDUM
These flowers offer nectar for tons of pollinators all summer long.

5 PENSTEMON
A wide array of kinds and hues make this tough perennial one to try.

generative cells fertilize the female egg cells in the ovules, which ripen into seeds.

Most flowers have both female and male parts, and self-pollination works just fine for many plants. But if one plant cross-pollinates with another of the same species, they will produce more robust offspring.

Different species have different ways of fostering cross-pollination unions. For example, a cucumber displays both male and female flowers on the same plant. In some plants, like holly and willows, flowers have only pistils or only stamens, and they must be cross-pollinated. Apple trees, too, require cross-pollination to produce fruit.

The Pollinators

The matchmakers are bees, butterflies, bugs and birds that become unwitting cupids when they visit flowers for food.

"Some pollinators eat parts of the flower itself," Matthew says. "Others seek the sugar-rich nectar or the protein- and amino acid-packed pollen, either to eat themselves or collect for their offspring."

To get at this meal, they must brush past the anthers and stigma, and in the process, they pick up and deliver pollen. You've likely seen hummingbirds and butterflies with a heavy dusting on their foreheads, or bees with pouches of the stuff clinging to their legs.

Flowers are designed to woo specific pollinators. For instance, bees and butterflies tend to swarm flowers with sweet aromas, but blooms that rely on hummingbirds for pollination typically have no scent and rely solely on color, particularly red. Tomato flowers have pollen that is difficult to detach from the anthers, so they rely on the buzzing of bumblebees to shake it loose.

The next time you see a bee light on a flower, take a moment to appreciate how much is going on to make sure both plant and pollinator continue to thrive.

American lady butterfly on zinnias

Positively *Peony*

Timeless and lovely, these plants are popular for a reason.

Do Tell peony

100

Plant a peony today: it may be around for generations. When planted and cared for correctly, these plants last as long as 100 years.

1980s

The commercial growth and public interest in peonies took a hit after World War II, though their popularity grew again starting in the 1980s.

1957

Indiana made the peony its official flower in 1957, awarding it the title the zinnia had held since 1931.

6

Per the American Peony Society, this garden favorite is available in six flowers: single, double, semi-double, anemone, bomb and Japanese.

270

The University of Michigan's Nichols Arboretum Peony Garden showcases more than 270 historic cultivars. Admission is free, so plan a peony visit during spring. The arboretum also offers other gardens and is open seven days a week.

40

For peonies to truly thrive, most varieties require an average winter temperature below 40 degrees. Chilly temps help the buds develop.

2

North America is home to two native peony species: *Paeonia brownii* and *P. californica*, and both can be found along the West Coast.

FLORIBUNDA
Floribundas, like Cinco de Mayo from David Austin, produce dense bloom clusters on one branch.

Coming Up *Roses*

From classic red blooming hybrids to sprawling pink climbers, these garden favorites come in all shapes and sizes. Before you toss any old rose plant into the ground, use this guide to find one that's a perfect fit for your space.

SHRUB
For blooms throughout the season, grow shrub roses like Pinktopia (above).

Shrub

Shrub types can grow upright, mounding or as ground covers. They're so easy to live with and care for that you may not even think of them as roses. Their genes protect against diseases and pests that typically plague other roses. Shrub roses are generally cold hardy and rebloom throughout the growing season. However, many shrub types carry little to no fragrance. If a sweet scent is important to you, check to see if fragrance is mentioned in the plant tag information, or buy one with a name that implies scent.

CLIMBER
Try this climbing Tess of the d'Urbervilles from David Austin. Plant a clematis vine nearby for a multi-flower display.

HYBRID TEA
Just Joey

MINIFLORA
First Impression

Grow shrub roses in masses or as companions to other plants, and choose from an array of colors, shapes and sizes. Brand names to look for include the Knock Out family of roses, Easy Elegance, Oso Easy and Oso Happy, David Austin, Griffith Buck, Kordes, Meidiland and Flower Carpet.

Miniature and Miniflora

Miniatures come as short as 6 inches or as tall as 3 feet, with small, hybrid tealike blooms that grow solo or in clusters. Miniflora roses feature compact plants—up to 3 feet tall—but grow full-size flowers as wide as 3 inches. Miniatures tuck well into the edges of flower borders and do well in pots. The term "patio rose" refers to any type of rose compact enough to grow in pots on a deck, not to a specific type of rose.

Hybrid Tea

With gorgeous, classic flowers and a perfumelike scent to swoon over, hybrid teas probably come to mind when you think of traditional roses. The plants grow 4 to 6 feet tall with strong canes (main branches) and individual blooms. The foliage, which often falls prey to diseases, doesn't cover the lower part of the canes, giving the plants a naked or barelegged look. If that's not your style, plant companion growers to help with screening the stalks. Hybrid teas require specific pruning regimens for best flowering. They prefer mild climates and need special protection in regions where winters are severe.

Climber and Rambler

Climbers are repeat bloomers; ramblers are not. They come from a wide range of rose types, but most are shrubs. Their canes—the thorny, woody stalks—stretch from 10 to more than 20 feet long. However, they must be lashed to supports with soft ties, since they can't hold on by themselves. It may take two to three years for climbers to mature and fill in. To promote better blooming, allow the canes coming from the base of the plant to grow to their full length. Keep the major ones as horizontal as possible to encourage better flowering as well as more shoots growing lower on the cane.

CLIMBER Lean a trellis against a structure to create a wall of blooms with varieties like this Zephirine Drouhin.

5 SECRETS FOR SUCCESS

Expert tips and tricks to grow your best roses yet.

1 Combine roses with other plants, including perennials, instead of isolating them. "Your garden should be an expression of what you want. There's no recipe for what to do," says Jacques Ferare, a vice president at Star Roses and Plants.

2 Shop for roses labeled "own root," which means they were grown from their own cuttings. Own-root roses survive cold winters and produce shoots from their own roots, leading to fuller, healthier plants.

3 Choose newer varieties that have been bred to need less care.

4 Find small sizes to grow in containers on a sunny patio or balcony. "They've been doing this in Europe for years," says Natalia Hamill of Bailey Nurseries.

5 Plant roses in full sun, where most of them bloom best—though you may find some that grow with as little as six hours of sun per day.

Floribunda and Grandiflora

Floribundas, also called spray roses, grow with several blooms in a rounded clump. Grandifloras resemble a blend of hybrid tea and floribunda roses, with large blooms produced both individually and in sprays. "You get the whole color scheme and look of a hybrid tea rose with shrub rose performance," says Natalia Hamill, a manager at Bailey Nurseries, which produces the Easy Elegance rose brands. Floribundas and grandifloras both produce blooms that are likely to have better fragrance than shrub roses.

Tree

Tree roses, or standards, are formal and traditional. They may be from almost any rose category. Several buds are grafted to a sturdy hybrid or hardy rose cane to give it the shape of a small tree. Some even come with two different kinds of roses grafted onto the same cane. Use standards as focal points, to line a path or as partners flanking doorways. Requiring staking and careful pruning, they work well in containers. If you're growing a tree rose in a cold climate, tuck it into a pot and overwinter it in an unheated space so it goes dormant but does not freeze.

The wind was light, the sun was full and this sunflower was at its peak. I like the way all of the contrasting elements in this photo, from lavender in the foreground to soft lights in the background, accentuate the strong yellow of the sunflower.

Tony Pocewicz CARPENTERSVILLE, ILLINOIS

Flowers *in Focus*

As the weather warms, green buds burst into vivid yellow sunflowers and perfectly pink roses. Bees, butterflies and other pollinators sporadically dance within the flowers, and fragrances fill the air. This season, spend some quality time among the blooms.

A nearby park was teeming with coneflowers, bee balm and many other blooms. I captured this hummingbird moth feasting on bee balm.

Ellen Enriquez
WAUKESHA, WISCONSIN

Every year,
I grow a variety of
sunflowers, and this
particular one came
back on its own.
Sunflowers aren't just
beautiful—they're highly
beneficial for bees, too.
The bee zooming toward
the open sunflower is
proof of that attraction!

Lorraine Lynch
PISCATAWAY, NEW JERSEY

Night-blooming cereus (sometimes called Queen of the Night) is a large cactus that flowers only once a year and dies the next morning when the sun comes up. Punahou School in Honolulu has rock walls that feature thousands of night-blooming cereus blossoms. It's a visual feast when they open in July and August.
Dwain Hansen HONOLULU, HAWAII

I've always loved
black-eyed Susans with their wide range of patterns and colors. When I spotted this one, lightly streaked with orange, I grabbed my camera to capture the way it peeked out from behind its yellow neighbors. It wasn't until later that I noticed the tiny bee busily gathering pollen.
Janine Heck
UNION, CONNECTICUT

My mom picked up this Holy Gate echeveria at a local greenhouse a couple of years ago. I had never seen anything like it and thought the vibrant red flowers were striking. Plus, the shape of the succulent here reminds me of a heart. I took the photo on my parents' back patio just before a thunderstorm.

Mike Droppleman
NORTON, OHIO

We live in the high desert, and in the spring, our backyard yucca trees start to sprout. This hesperoyucca is about two weeks from full maturity, when it will finish as a beautiful lightbulb-shaped flower. I was delighted to see that I captured a little hitchhiker ladybug in the photo.

Deborah Saldana
OAK HILLS, CALIFORNIA

The first year I grew zinnias,

I fell in love! I took many photos from nearly every angle. Two years later, this is still one of my favorite shots, because it's a pretty yet unexpected perspective. I also like the outlining on the bottom of the zinnias and the way it creates a sharp contrast with the light green stalk and the pink petals. Here in the Dallas area, zinnias often last into November and provide nectar to monarchs migrating south.

Lana Dion
GARLAND, TEXAS

When I think of beautiful

flowers, my mind does not immediately go to fruit, but when I saw a pineapple blooming with such stunning colors, I had to photograph it. Pineapple plants can be a bit thorny, and it was difficult to get a good shot from the side. When I looked down from the top, though, I knew I'd found the best possible angle.

Elaine Mancusi
PORT ST. LUCIE, FLORIDA

I noticed that if I looked through the green spiral of this corkscrew rush, it framed the vinca bloom perfectly. It reminded me how much natural beauty there is in the world. I really like the way the connection between these two simple plants creates a whole new elegance.

Jason Justice
MORROW, OHIO

When I first began dabbling in photography, I thought I'd end up focusing on landscapes or wildlife. One day during a trip to Scotland, I snapped this picture of foxglove after a fresh morning rain. It was one of the first photos I took specifically of a plant, and when I saw how much detail and beauty was reflected in the image, I knew flower photography would become my new passion.

Jennifer Cleary
CHESAPEAKE CITY, MARYLAND

Nature's beautiful colors return to the Midwest each spring. While I visited family, I noticed their gardens were in full bloom. This marguerite daisy is a perfect example. I love its color and detail.

Jacob Sewell MUNCIE, INDIANA

Houseplant *Heroes*

Add a burst of flowering color to your indoor space.

1

1 Begonia
BEGONIA

With tons of begonia options, it's hard to choose just one. Wax begonias are the classic choice, with sturdy leaves and lots of flowers. Angel wing and rex begonias add interesting foliage into the mix. All begonias like a little extra humidity, so fill a shallow dish with water and rocks and set the pot on top.

Why we love it: Double begonias boast blooms that look like roses, and petals on picotee types have darker edges that make them stand out.

2 Chinese hibiscus
HIBISCUS ROSA-SINENSIS

Nothing evokes the feeling of sunny climates like the big, bright blossoms of tropical hibiscus. Give it plenty of room to grow along with as much direct sun as possible, and you'll reap the rewards all year long. Hibiscus blooms on new growth, so prune it only once or twice a year.

Why we love it: New cultivars offer stunning blossoms in an array of colors, and the double-flowered varieties amp up the wow factor.

3 Kalanchoe
KALANCHOE BLOSSFELDIANA

Kalanchoe (say "kal-un-KOH-ee") is a short-day plant; it needs 14 hours of total darkness each night to start blooming. Look for bunches of red, orange, pink or white to appear among the waxy green leaves by the end of February. Kalanchoe is a succulent, so occasional thorough watering is all it requires.

Why we love it: Late winter is when we tend to need a colorful display the most, so kalanchoe's long-lasting clusters of starry blooms show up at the perfect time.

4 African violet
SAINTPAULIA

This quintessential flowering houseplant has a few quirks. Use room-temperature water to wet the soil when dry, but don't let drops stay on leaves or allow the roots to sit in water. African violets require lots of bright indirect light, but be sure to keep your plant out of direct sun. Once you've figured out the right location, you'll know—a blooming African violet is a happy one.

Why we love it: Successful plants make multiple crowns that you can remove and use to grow new plants for friends.

6 Flowering maple
ABUTILON PICTUM

This houseplant is a member of the mallow family. Flowering maple has lovely bell-shaped blossoms in shades of yellow, orange and white. Popular in Victorian times, this unusual small shrub is making a much-deserved comeback. Give it lots of sun indoors; move it outside for the summer.

Why we love it: Varieties like Tiger Eye offer striking yellow blooms with red veins, and the maplelike leaves add interest year-round.

7 Jasmine
JASMINUM POLYANTHUM

Your home will feel like spring when this fragrant favorite bursts into delicate bloom. The tiny white flowers pack a perfumed punch that continues for weeks, turning your home into a sweetly scented paradise. Jasmine needs lower night temperatures to flower, so keep it away from furnace vents.

Why we love it: Jasmine is a vine, so use it in hanging pots or place a small decorative trellis in the container and train it to climb.

5 Geranium
PELARGONIUM

Scented geraniums have been treasured houseplants since colonial days, when housewives shared cuttings to brighten neighbors' homes. Ivy-leaved geraniums spill over the sides of their containers, while seed and zonal geraniums are more upright.

Why we love it: A well-cared-for heirloom geranium survives for years, and easy propagation from cuttings makes sharing with friends a snap.

8 Lipstick plant
AESCHYNANTHUS RADICANS

The flower clusters on the lipstick plant are sure to draw admiring eyes. The small scarlet flower rises from a maroon tube-shaped bud, looking just like the lipstick it's named for. This tropical vine prefers bright light, regular fertilizer and soil kept moist but not wet.

Why we love it: Hang a lipstick plant in a brightly lit room and let the flower-covered vines trail down.

9

9 Orchid
ORCHIDACEAE FAMILY

With orchids, it's best to start out easy with a Phalaenopsis, which is also called a moth orchid. These low-maintenance beauties thrive in any light except direct sun and, in general, only need weekly watering. Other popular varieties of orchids include Cattleya and Dendrobium.
Why we love it: Orchid blooms last for weeks or months with minimal care, and some are wonderfully fragrant.

10 Amaryllis
HIPPEASTRUM

Bearing multiple buds on a single stalk, the amaryllis is a popular holiday gift. They flower only once a year, but these showstoppers are worth the wait. When the display is over, cut off the stalks and allow the foliage to grow. New buds will appear the following winter.
Why we love it: Horticulturalists have created dozens of amaryllis specimens, and they're all easy to maintain.

10

The *Power* of *Shrubs*

Whether it's structure, privacy, color or wildlife you want, it's easy to find the perfect bush for the garden.

GROWING ON A SMALLER SCALE than trees, shrubs are easier to manage and more admirable at eye level. Their size also means it's easier to find spots for them in an existing landscape, and they won't create large areas of unwanted shade. Follow these simple steps and put shrubs to work for you.

Be a Savvy Shopper

First find out which shrubs meet your needs. Maybe you're looking for foundation plantings around your house, a colorful autumnal show, security around windows or varieties that produce berries for birds. Whatever you need, ask the experts at your local nursery, check plant tags, surf the internet, consult reference books or page through garden magazines for recommendations.

Another option is to talk to your neighbors, especially those with shrubs you've admired. Ask them which varieties they grow or where they purchased them. The advantage is that you already know it grows well in your area.

Invincibelle Mini Mauvette hydrangea is new on the garden scene. Deep pink blooms return on this dwarf grower every year and persist most of the season. The dwarf habit makes it ideal for any landscape.

5 SHRUB STARS

These popular, easy-to-grow picks offer moderate height and colorful blooms—perfect for any yard.

1 Hydrangea

Bloom time: Summer.
Hardiness: Zones 3 to 9.
Flower color: Pink, white or blue.
Height: 3 to 22 feet.
Width: Up to 8 feet.
Light needs: Sun to shade.
Planting: Place in a hole the same depth as the root ball, but wider. Water thoroughly, keeping the soil moist but not soggy.

2 Rose of Sharon

Bloom time: Late summer to midautumn.
Hardiness: Zones 5 to 9.
Flower color: Pink, red, purple, blue or white.
Height: 8 to 12 feet.
Width: 6 to 8 feet.
Light needs: Full sun to partial shade.
Planting: In northern areas, plant in spring. Thrives in moist soil that drains well.

Find the Right Spot

Take a walk around your property and determine where shrubs may fit in. Where are there gaps? Where would brilliant color or the special form of a shrub be welcome? The best time to assess these questions is before or after perennials and annuals have had their glory days. That way, you're not distracted by their beautiful shows.

"Extend your annual budget by prioritizing planting projects," says horticulture expert Melinda Myers. "Focus on the areas that will provide the greatest benefits."

The next step is figuring out how to make room for them. One way is to replace any current shrubs you don't like. If they're overgrown or they no longer excite you, it may be time to make way for something new.

Look for spots that can easily accommodate a new shrub. Check out the back of a flower border, for example. Install a hedge as a boundary line. Or cover up your home's foundation or the lower part of a deck.

Another option is to steal some lawn. Every keen gardener has probably already done this once or twice. Making your lawn smaller by digging up some more turf even reduces regular upkeep!

As you search for the perfect spot, pay attention to the light. Most shrubs require sun or part shade to thrive. If you have large trees nearby, their canopies can stunt the growth of many shrubs and also create problems with competing root systems. Most often, the long-established trees win.

However, fully exposed areas leave shrubs vulnerable. Full-on bright sun can bleach-out leaf and flower color, especially in the South. Most shrubs do well in more moderate light conditions. Give them a break from the blazing heat of midday, whether it's the shadow of your house or garage, or the dappled shade of nearby trees.

Before you break ground, verify that the site is sheltered from the wind. Full gusts stress the plants, causing them to wilt and struggle. Plus windy conditions strip away the desired foliage.

Finally, consider the shrub's eventual size (find it on the plant tag), and give it room to grow.

3 Mountain Laurel

Bloom time: Spring to midsummer.
Hardiness: Zones 4 to 9.
Flower color: Pink, white or red.
Height: 5 to 15 feet.
Width: 5 to 15 feet.
Light needs: Full sun to shade (best flowers in sunnier locations).

Planting: Plant in moist, acidic, well-draining soils for best results.

4 Camellia

Bloom time: Winter to early spring.
Hardiness: Zones 6 to 11.
Flower color: Red, pink or white.
Height: 3 to 20 feet.
Width: 3 to 20 feet.
Light needs: Partial shade.
Planting: Plant root ball even with surrounding soil. To keep roots moist, cover them with 2 inches of mulch.

5 Forsythia

Bloom time: Early to midspring.
Hardiness: Zones 3 to 8.
Flower color: Yellow.
Height: 1 to 10 feet.
Width: 3 to 10 feet.
Light needs: Full sun.
Planting: Plant in a hole as deep as, but wider than, the root ball. Space plants 2½ to 6 feet apart.

Start Planting

Now it's time to plant! Remove all tags, wires or ropes from your shrub's stems or trunk. Dig a hole at least two times wider than the diameter of the root ball, but no deeper than the height of the entire root system.

Before placing your plant, remove any large rocks and debris before scratching the sides of the planting hole with your shovel. This makes it easier for roots to penetrate the surrounding soil.

Since roots extend well beyond the planting hole, there's no need to amend the soil. Besides, if a plant's roots enjoy the rich soil too much, they stay within the planting hole, eventually becoming root bound.

Loosen the roots of pot-bound, container-grown shrubs. Ease the plant out of the pot, and use a sharp knife to make four slices in the root mass, from top to bottom at even intervals, about an inch deep. This severs any strangling roots and inspires new growth.

Place the shrub at the same depth it was while growing in the container. "Look for the crown—the place where stems meet the roots on the shrub," says Melinda. "Remove excess soil to expose the crown. Keep it at the soil surface for the health and longevity of the shrub." Next,

backfill with the existing soil, and water the shrub heavily to eliminate air pockets. Finish filling the hole to ground level. Use any excess soil to build a ring about 6 inches from the outside edge of the hole, creating a watering moat.

Finishing Touches

Add enough water to moisten the top 6 to 12 inches of soil. Keep the root zone moist but not soggy.

Shrubs need thorough but infrequent watering. Check newly planted shrubs in sandy soils or hot regions twice a week. Those in clay soils or cooler regions should be checked every seven to 10 days.

Apply a layer of organic mulch around new plantings. It helps conserve moisture and moderate the soil temperature. Just be careful not to pile mulch over the crowns of plants.

"New plantings look sparse when you properly space young shrubs in the garden bed," Melinda says. "For instant beauty with long-term benefits, fill the voids with annuals or perennials. As your shrubs grow, fewer annuals are needed each year, and the perennials can eventually be moved to a new location."

PHOTOS
of the
YEAR

Enjoy these gorgeous shots from the past year of *Birds & Blooms* magazine. Go to *birdsandblooms.com/ submit* to contribute.

1 Lotus flower
Cindy Knapp
SAN DIEGO, CALIFORNIA

2 Strawflower
Carol Milisen
WOODLAND PARK,
COLORADO

3 Sunflower
Nicole Faulkner
BRANDON, MISSISSIPPI

CHAPTER 7

Butterflies & BUGS

Attract and identify some of the most beautiful and amazing backyard creatures.

Butterfly Season

Readers capture the magical moments when these charming fliers stop for a photo op.

EASTERN TIGER SWALLOWTAIL

I found this butterfly frolicking about in a field of
brilliant sunflowers in Meigs County, Tennessee.
Its stunning open wings, with so many shades of
yellow, perfectly complement the hues of the flower,
while the blues balance the color of the vibrant sky.
—*Denise Neuendorf, Cleveland, Tennessee*

CHECKERED WHITE

It was sunny and 80 degrees the day I captured this shot. I was photographing my friend's sunflower field in Hudson, Maryland, when I noticed the many varieties of butterflies that also were there. I saw this checkered white—plus tiger swallowtails, monarchs and cloudless sulphurs.

—*Lori Bramble, Cambridge, Maryland*

COMMON BUCKEYE

This photo is of a pretty little common buckeye butterfly. It was enjoying the goldenrod flowers that grow wild in an area of my yard that I choose not to mow.

—*Laura Frazier, Kearneysville, West Virginia*

PAINTED LADY

I grew Mexican sunflowers, and they did not disappoint! The blooms attracted many varieties of butterflies, bees and hummingbirds. I spotted this pair of busy painted ladies nectaring on the flowers. There seems to be a lot of these beautiful fliers in my neck of the woods.

—*Kathleen Otto, Lawrence, Kansas*

GREAT SPANGLED FRITILLARY

Several great spangled fritillaries sipped nectar from a milkweed plant in my garden. The orange and black markings on their upper wings are so striking, and I like how you can see the white spots only on the underside of their wings.

—*Kevin O'Gara, Pleasant Valley, Connecticut*

WHITE PEACOCK

The white peacock butterfly is one of my favorites. This one posed very nicely on a leaf, and my lens caught the powdery wings, bright colors, and even the fuzzy thorax and abdomen.

—*Jennifer Torrance, Pittsburgh, Pennsylvania*

MONARCH

It's always a special treat when monarch butterflies arrive at my pear tree. While in the yard, I always carry my Nikon D5500 camera because you never know when a beautiful creature will appear. My camera is set on continuous shooting to capture every moment.

—*Ginger English, Bauxite, Arkansas*

KARNER BLUE

Wild lupine grows at the Wilton Wildlife Preserve & Park near my home, and it attracts karner blue butterflies, a species I have always wanted to see. I was amazed at how tiny the butterfly is—only thumbnail size. I had originally been looking for something a lot larger.
—*Deborah Bryk, Saratoga Springs, New York*

ZEBRA SWALLOWTAIL

This butterfly's markings really stood out to me. I haven't seen many zebra swallowtails, so I was very excited to capture one in this photo. It took several tries to get one with the wings open. The wait was well-worth it! I love how its orange antennae stand out against the background.
—*Cassie Brooke, Carbondale, Illinois*

BLACK SWALLOWTAIL
My grandmother gave me a start of gooseneck loosestrife several years ago, and the butterflies absolutely adore it. I love how the delicate white blooms look against the dark black butterfly. And the wing colors are so vibrant and pretty.
—*Amy Tipton, Erwin, Tennessee*

Butterflies *On the Move*

Use host plants to make sure your backyard is ready for any migrating flier that stops by.

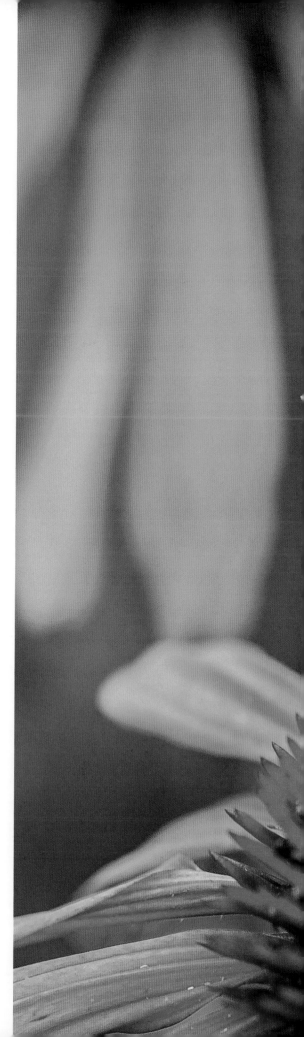

EACH YEAR, MILLIONS OF monarch butterflies make an epic journey to Mexico in fall and retrace their paths back north in spring. To aid them, gardeners all over the country are restoring monarch habitat. However, some other migratory butterflies need your help, too.

Painted ladies move in response to changes in the environment, such as heavy winter rains that spark the growth of host plants in desert regions. They gather in such large numbers for these journeys that they've even shown up on weather radar in a swath more than 70 miles wide! Painted lady migrations are well-known in certain areas, including the western United States. It's hard to predict when they will happen, but the number of participants is massive. These migrating butterflies are found all over the world, making them one of the most widespread species.

A SIGHT TO SEE

In the summer of 2017, gardeners across the U.S. were unexpectedly treated to massive numbers of painted lady butterflies as the creatures migrated.

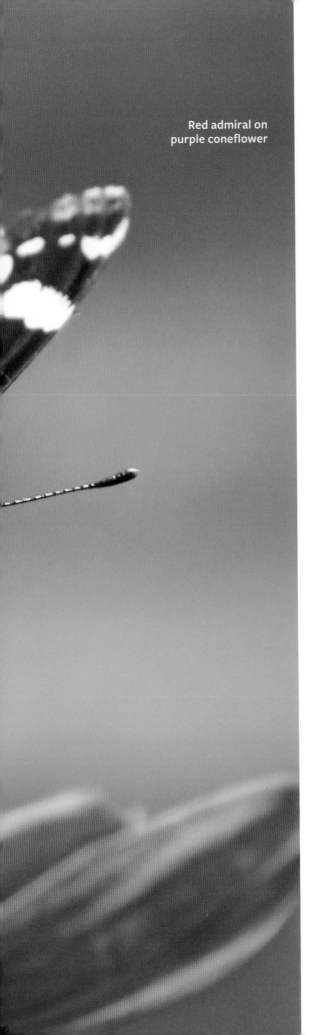

Red admiral on purple coneflower

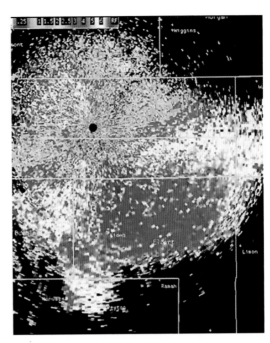

SO MANY BUTTERFLIES!

This radar image captured a group of migrating painted lady butterflies flying over Colorado.

Red admiral butterflies also migrate. Seen throughout much of the country by midsummer, they are unable to survive freezing temperatures during their life cycle. Northern populations die off in the fall, and those areas are repopulated the next summer by the year-round breeding population from the southern states. While the migration of red admirals is less visually impressive than that of painted ladies, it's easily tracked as they spread north from Texas each spring. Other butterflies that migrate north from a southern breeding population each year include cloudless sulphurs and common buckeyes.

How You Can Help

Of course, butterflies can only make these amazing journeys when they have access to food and shelter along the way. With so much of their native habitat destroyed by development,

MIGRATION IN A NUTSHELL

It occurs when large numbers of animals travel from one area to another. Movement during migration is purposeful. Other than stopping to rest and feed, the animals continue their quest until they reach their final destination.

Cloudless sulphur
on plumbago

butterflies depend more than ever on gardens with host plants. Support healthy populations by making your backyard the best possible wildlife habitat it can be.

Helping them will help your yard, too, says Rhiannon Crain, project director for the Habitat Network, a joint project of the Nature Conservancy and the Cornell Lab of Ornithology. "Butterflies are such pivotal organisms in our backyard life cycles. They help pollinate as adults and serve as a food source for birds. Caterpillars keep plants in check even while they refresh the soil with their droppings. If you have a diversity of butterflies and moths in your garden, chances are you're doing something right."

Start improving your environment at the Habitat Network's website (*content.yardmap. org*), where you can map your yard, indicating all the trees, plants and wildlife features you have. Then use the site analysis tool, which Rhiannon says takes the map of your yard and analyzes it

Comma butterfly
on black-eyed
Susan perch

Question mark
butterfly with
pickerelweed

Common buckeye
pair resting on
blanket flowers

MEET THE NONMIGRANTS

A few butterflies, such as mourning cloaks, question marks and commas, completely shut down their bodies and hibernate through winter as adults. Most species survive the cold months as caterpillars, chrysalides or eggs. Only a few migrate to escape the winter weather.

HOST PLANT GUIDE

Create a backyard butterfly haven when you grow plants that caterpillars need most.

BUTTERFLY	HOST PLANT(S)
Red admiral	Nettles, pellitory
Painted lady	Thistles, hollyhock, mallow
Cloudless sulphur	Cassia
Question mark	Elm, hackberry, nettles
Common buckeye	Plantain, snapdragon, toadflax
Gulf fritillary	Passion vine

based on your goals. "If you want to garden for pollinators, we'll tell you what you are already doing right, and suggest some additional actions for you to consider," she says. Actions you may want to take include:

•**Adding early- and late-blooming nectar plants** to give butterflies energy throughout their most active seasons.

•**Choosing native host plants** to help support new generations.

•**Providing shelter for insects,** such as brush piles, dead tree snags or rock piles. (Avoid butterfly houses, which usually just turn into homes for wasps.)

•**Limiting pesticides in your garden.** Many kill all bugs indiscriminately. Instead, treat serious problems on a case-by-case basis.

•**Keeping your yard a little messy and leaving leaf litter** for butterflies to tuck themselves inside to overwinter as caterpillars or chrysalides.

Your Garden Matters

Migratory butterflies make some of the most impressive journeys on earth. They float on delicate wings for hundreds or thousands of miles, fueled only by flower nectar and a compelling impulse to continue their flight. As butterfly habitats decline and unpredictable weather patterns create new challenges, their travels become more difficult. Those of us who love these creatures must keep doing our best to help them along the way.

Grow hollyhocks and get ready to watch hungry painted lady caterpillars munch on the large leaves.

A Monarch *Mimic*

Learn how viceroy butterflies are masters of disguise.

IT HAPPENS TO EVERY NATURE enthusiast at least once. You spot an orange butterfly with black markings hovering around a flower and say, "Oh, look, it's a monarch!" Except, on closer inspection, you realize it's not. That bold beauty is actually one of the monarch mimics—a viceroy.

Once you know how to spot the difference, it's easy to tell the two apart. Generally, viceroys are a bit smaller than monarchs. But the simplest way to differentiate between them is to check for the extra black line that extends all the way across the lower wing. You can see this giveaway whether the wings are open or closed.

Mimicry is a common form of defense among butterflies. Both monarchs and viceroys eat plants that contain bitter-tasting chemicals. For the monarchs, it's milkweed, which contains toxic latex sap. Monarchs have learned to tolerate it and store those toxins in their bodies to make them taste bad to predators, both as caterpillars and adults.

Likewise, viceroy caterpillars consume host plants in the willow family that contain salicylic acids, and viceroys store them in their bodies, just as monarchs store latex sap. By evolving to resemble each other, monarchs and viceroys signal to predators that they're both unpalatable.

Viceroys mimic other monarch look-alikes, too. Queen and soldier butterflies have darker, burnt orange-brown coloring compared to monarchs. They're only found in southern areas. Viceroys that also live in the South are noticeably darker than those in northern regions, as they mimic the queen instead of the monarch.

Viceroy caterpillars look nothing like their yellow, white and black-striped monarch counterparts. Instead, in their later stages and in chrysalis, they mimic a pile of bird droppings—clearly not a tasty meal!

Unlike monarchs, viceroys don't migrate, and adults die off before winter sets in. When the days grow short, late-season caterpillars use silk to secure leaf stems firmly to branches. They roll up the leaves and shelter inside through winter. As soon as fresh leaves grow in spring, the caterpillars emerge and resume eating. In just a few weeks, new adults appear.

Viceroys are found in or near wetlands and moist woodlands throughout most of the United States and parts of Canada and Mexico. Adults sip nectar from flowers but also love rotting fruit and tree sap, especially in spring. You can attract them to your backyard garden by planting their host plants, such as willow, cottonwood and poplar.

BACKYARD DECODER

Figure out whether a viceroy or monarch is visiting your garden.

VICEROY	CHARACTERISTIC	MONARCH
Black line across lower wing on both sides	WING PATTERN	No black line on either side of lower wing
2 ½ to 3 ½ inches	WINGSPAN	3 ½ to 5 inches
Willow, poplar, cottonwood	HOST PLANT	Milkweed

BRUSHFOOTS

WINGSPAN: $\frac{7}{8}$ TO 4 INCHES

The brushfoot (Nymphalidae) family gets its name from the short hairs covering the tiny front legs of its members. A diverse range of fliers are part of this group, including fritillaries, admirals, crescents and monarchs.

Painted ladies

Boost Your *Butterfly ID*

Learn which family your backyard flier belongs to with this guide.

American copper

Eastern tiger swallowtail

Orange sulphur

GOSSAMER-WINGED

WINGSPAN: $\frac{2}{3}$ TO 2 INCHES

Four distinct North American groups are part of the Lycaenidae family: coppers, hairstreaks, harvesters and blues. Many in the gossamer-winged group have eyespots as well as short extensions on their hindwings to fool predators into grabbing the wrong end, which makes escape easier.

SWALLOWTAILS

WINGSPAN: 2 TO 5 INCHES

The biggest butterflies in North America are part of the swallowtail (Papilionidae) family. Their most familiar members are the eastern and western tigers, which, like most swallowtails, have a long taillike extension on both hindwings. But some species in this family are tailless, notably the parnassians.

WHITES AND SULPHURS

WINGSPAN: 1 TO 3 INCHES

If you've seen a dainty white or yellow butterfly visiting your flower garden, it's probably a member of the Pieridae family, which includes whites, sulphurs and orangetips. Some southern members of this group wander far north in summer and fall.

Tigers in Flight

ID eastern tiger swallowtails.

Thin yellow and black body

Wingspan ranges from 3½ to 5 inches

Black and yellow tiger stripes on wings (on some females, black with shadow stripes)

Blue marking near the bottom of the tail (females have more blue spots)

Yellow dots and dashes outline the wings

Signature three-lobed hindwings

THREE TIGERS
Eastern, western and Canadian tiger swallowtail butterflies look almost identical, but the latter two are smaller. Use geography to tell them apart. Western tigers are found from the Rocky Mountains westward; eastern tigers from the Great Plains eastward; and Canadian tigers in central New England, New York, Michigan, Minnesota, Montana and northward.

Western tiger swallowtail

Welcome, *Caterpillars*

Grow host plants to help the next generation of
butterflies and moths survive and thrive.

1

**WORTH
THE WAIT**
Gas plants may
take a few years to
get established, but
the showy result is
so rewarding.

1 Gas plant

DICTAMNUS ALBUS, ZONES 3 TO 8

This novelty plant is a stunner. From May to June, white, pink or lilac flowers top vertical stems that reach 3 feet tall. The plant is low maintenance but needs full sun and well-draining soil. Wear gloves when handling gas plants to avoid any adverse skin reactions.

Why we love it: On windless summer nights, light the flammable oil from the gas plant's old flowers or seedpods to emit a brief vapor.

Host to: giant swallowtail

2 Little bluestem

SCHIZACHYRIUM SCOPARIUM, ZONES 3 TO 9

A blue-stemmed beauty, this tufted warm-season grass provides wonderful winter interest. It's also a resilient host plant that grows best on dry upland sites such as hilltops or ridges, although it is very adaptable to nearly all soil conditions.

Why we love it: The USDA says little bluestem is one of the best grasses for nesting and roosting birds, such as finches, sparrows and juncos.

Host to: common wood-nymphs and skippers

Giant swallowtail

3 Prairie blazing star

LIATRIS PYCNOSTACHYA, ZONES 3 TO 9

In late summer and autumn, blazing star's radiant rose-purple flowers spike skyward, providing vivid color in your backyard. This hardy prairie favorite can grow up to 4 feet tall, especially if it is in a damp environment.

Why we love it: It's a low-maintenance, plant-it-and-leave-it bloom that reseeds readily, and it makes excellent fresh-cut flowers.

Host to: glorious flower moth

4 Pale purple coneflower

ECHINACEA PALLIDA, ZONES 4 TO 8

This alluring wildflower grows about 3 feet tall, and during its late spring to midsummer bloom show, the flower heads sprout pale purple petals that are about 3 inches long.

Why we love it: Many gardeners pop pale purple coneflowers into the garden just for the long showy flower heads.

Host to: silvery checkerspot

5 Saskatoon serviceberry

AMELANCHIER ALNIFOLIA, ZONES 3 TO 8

The Saskatoon serviceberry is an ornamental shrub that produces white flowers in spring and purple-black berries in early summer. This plant usually grows 3 to 8 feet tall and requires full sun or light shade.

Why we love it: The berries are tasty in pies and muffins—if you can beat the robins to them.

Host to: Canadian tiger swallowtail and pale swallowtail

6 Spice bush

LINDERA BENZOIN, ZONES 4 TO 9

In fall, the nicely shaped shrub's blooms and its shiny red berries produce a sweet, spicy fragrance. About 6 to 12 feet tall when fully grown, this hardy host is commonly found in low woods, swampy areas and along streams.

Why we love it: Wood thrushes and more than 20 other bird species flock to backyards to gobble up the juicy red berries.

Host to: spicebush swallowtail and other swallowtails

7 Common hop

HUMULUS LUPULUS, ZONES 3 TO 8

Craft beer lovers, rejoice! This host has been used to brew beer for more than 1,200 years. Plant common hop in sandy, well-draining soil, and make sure there's plenty of room because this vine grows up to 26 feet long. It always winds clockwise and has a root system up to 16 feet deep.

Why we love it: Historically, this plant is important. Native Americans used it to induce sleep and treat rheumatism, pneumonia and nervousness.

Host to: eastern comma and question mark

8 Buttonbush

CEPHALANTHUS OCCIDENTALIS, ZONES 3 TO 11

Buttonbush is a hardy shrub that grows 6 to 12 feet tall, especially when planted in shade and wet soil. "This is one I think more people should be growing," says Dan Scott, associate director of gardens and facilities at the American Horticultural Society. "It presents an incredible white pincushion-esque flower in midsummer."

Why we love it: Ducks and shorebirds eat the seeds.

Host to: hydrangea sphinx, titan sphinx and royal walnut moth

9

Viceroy butterfly

9 Rattlesnake master

ERYNGIUM YUCCIFOLIUM, ZONES 4 TO 9

Ominously named, this plant is known for its 1-inch, orb-shaped clusters of many small flowers. Whitish bracts stick out sharply from the flowers, giving the head a rough, prickly look and feel. This warm-season perennial grows best in dry prairie soil.

Why we love it: The heads give off a honeylike odor when in bloom from June to September.

Host to: rattlesnake-master borer moth.

10 Blue grama

BOUTELOUA GRACILIS, ZONES 3 TO 10

Blue grama is a graceful grass that grows readily on the Great Plains but is tough enough for other zones. Once established, this warm-season grass reaches 2 feet tall, prefers dry soils and needs lots of sun.

Why we love it: Its seed head is eyelashlike and extraordinary, but the real beauty of blue grama is that it's so easy to maintain.

Host to: skippers and skipperlings

Male ebony
jewelwing
damselfly

DID YOU KNOW?

Damselflies and
dragonflies have been
around for more than
200 million years. They
once flew among the
dinosaurs and were
intimidating forces
to be reckoned with.
Back then, some of the
dragonflies were super-
sized and measured
almost 3 feet long!

Flying *Jewels*

Gain a newfound appreciation for iridescent damselflies.

BLINK AND YOU MIGHT MISS 'EM! Less than 3 inches long with thin, delicate bodies, damselflies glide through gardens in search of small flying insects.

Damselflies and dragonflies both come from the same Odonata order (referred to collectively as odonates), but damselflies have noticeably thinner bodies. Damselflies choose from the same menu as dragonflies, but they focus on the smallest items, eating tiny insects like gnats, mosquitoes and midges.

The diversity of colors damselflies display is impressive. Blues and greens are most common, but some species are red, orange or yellow. Coloration often differs between males and females. For example, male bluets are blue, while females may be blue, green or brown.

A backyard water feature such as a shallow pond helps attract damselflies to your landscape by luring the insects they eat. Otherwise, find these odonates near wetlands and other fresh water. Look for perched damselflies soaking up the morning sun, holding their wings close to their bodies. After they're warmed up, they take to the air in search of a meal of fresh insects.

Mating damselflies connect in wheel- or heart-shaped postures. They lay their eggs in shallow water; once hatched, the aquatic nymphs feed on small bugs. In its larval stage, a damselfly molts many times under water before moving on to land, where it transforms into a winged adult.

More than 5,000 species of odonates are spread across six continents; Antarctica is too cold for them. In the eastern United States, a widespread and easily recognizable species is the brilliant jade-bodied ebony jewelwing damselfly. The females lack the luster of the males but sport a white spot on each of their solid black wings.

Dancers, another common damselfly group, sometimes are found near slow-moving streams. Keep an eye out for blue-fronted dancers in the East and vivid dancers in the West.

Blue dasher dragonfly

DAMSELS VERSUS DRAGONS

Learn to spot the differences between these two flying insects.

DAMSELFLY	CHARACTERISTIC	DRAGONFLY
thin body	**BODY**	thick body
wings usually held straight back and above body	**WINGS**	open wings, spread out from the sides of the body
wide-set eyes on sides of head	**EYES**	large eyes nearly touch on top of head

The best way to examine odonates is to watch them through binoculars when they are perched. If you don't have a pair handy, you can still see them easily if you find a spot where they're active and simply wait. Don't worry; damselflies don't sting or bite. By sitting there patiently you'll get a true sense of their amazing world as damselflies cruise the vegetation for their next meal.

The Great *Sphinxes*

Watch for these moths as they mimic hummingbird behaviors.

White-lined sphinx moth

Snowberry clearwing

2

Of the four hummingbird moths in the sphinx family, only two are commonly seen—the hummingbird clearwing and the snowberry clearwing.

5

Five-spotted hawk moth caterpillars, also known as tomato hornworms, are driven by voracious appetites to feast on tomato, tobacco and potato plants.

30

Though not a bird (or a plane), sphinx moths move quickly. Snowberry clearwings have been clocked flying more than 30 mph.

11

A sphinx moth's proboscis (tongue that sips nectar) may be more than 11 inches long on some large tropical species.

6

The wingspan of sphinx moths varies by species. Big poplars spread their wings 4 to 6 inches, while smaller sphinxes, like hummingbird clearwings, open to about 2 inches.

4

Just like the fliers they resemble, sphinx moths prefer nectar-filled, tube-shaped flowers. Try these four: daturas, columbines, four-o'clocks and flowering tobacco.

A *Good* Bug

Learn this native ladybug's distinctive markings, and look for it in your garden.

Antennae, near the eyes, help poor-sighted ladybugs smell, taste and feel their way around.

Pronotum is a platelike structure that protects the ladybug's head. It has two white dashes on top.

Short legs secrete poisonous gel if the bug is caught by a predator.

The convergent lady beetle (shown here) eats pesky insects in gardens throughout North America.

Hard shells (elytra) cover and protect the wings. Dots on the left are a mirror image of those on the right.

Black spots on the orange shell alert predators that this creature tastes bad.

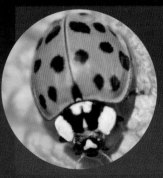

THE NOT-SO-GOOD KIND
Our native ladybugs are welcome guests in gardens, backyards and farm fields because they nosh on plant-eating insects, like aphids. It's their nonnative look-alikes, such as the Asian multicolored lady beetle (left), that have a bad reputation. They're the bothersome creatures that nudge their way into the warmth of your home. The Asian multicolored lady beetle has a black "M" on its pronotum.

PHOTOS
of the
YEAR

Enjoy these gorgeous shots from the past year of *Birds & Blooms* magazine. Go to *birdsandblooms.com/ submit* to contribute.

1 American Lady
Katerina Kretsch
BRISTOL, CONNECTICUT

2 Pearl Crescent
Leonora Bridges
FERRUM, VIRGINIA

3 Painted Lady
John Van Stelten
LOUISVILLE, COLORADO

4 Monarch
Terry Stanfill
GENTRY, ARKANSAS

Ask the EXPERTS

Get the best backyard advice on bird-watching from Kenn and Kimberly Kaufman and on gardening from Melinda Myers.

CHAPTER 8

A great spangled fritillary butterfly sits on milkweed flowers.

Q I picked about 100 milkweed seedpods. How do I get them to grow? Someone told me to spread them over mulch and lightly work them in. **Steve Ripp** NEENAH, WISCONSIN

Melinda: Many gardeners have found collecting and growing milkweed plants from seed a bit challenging. The seeds must be mature to sprout, so collect seeds from pods just before or as the pods split open. Increase your chance of success by removing seeds from the pod. Separate the seed from the fluff and store in the refrigerator or an airtight container for several months. This cold treatment is needed to end dormancy and increase sprouting success. Sow seeds indoors in a quality potting or seed-starting mix. Move the transplants into the garden after the danger of frost ends. You can also plant seeds directly outdoors in the fall.

Q I'd like to make homemade suet. Do you have a recipe? **Shirley Hrobar** TOMBALL, TEXAS

Kenn and Kimberly: Making suet can be messy but cost-effective and fun. Start with a general base by combining and melting 1 cup of peanut butter and 1 cup of lard over low heat. In a large glass bowl, mix 2 cups of quick oats, 2 cups of your favorite birdseed mix, 1 cup of yellow cornmeal and 1 cup of flour. Stir the melted ingredients into the dry mix and blend well.

Once the mixture has cooled a bit, press into molds (try cat food or tuna cans, or form into your favorite shape) and refrigerate. You may need to experiment with the ratio of ingredients to avoid crumbly cakes. It's OK to be creative and experiment with additional ingredients such as fruit and even dried mealworms. But do avoid bacon grease, bread, table scraps and honey.

A red-bellied woodpecker perches on a suet cage.

Irises

Q If different varieties of daylilies or irises are planted close together, will each plant continue to stay true to its original form? If not, how far apart should the plants be?

Barbara Wells MARINETTE, WISCONSIN

Melinda: The original plants will stay the same but due to cross-pollination (exchange of genetic material between two different varieties of daylily or iris), their offspring won't. You can avoid this problem by deadheading the faded flowers. This prevents seeds from developing. Also remove any unwanted seedlings that appear at the base of the plants (there won't be many). Don't worry about limiting growth. Both daylilies and irises increase in size as they grow larger root systems or rhizomes that produce more stems.

When growing daylilies or irises, it's possible to mix varieties, but stay with plants that are equally assertive. Otherwise, the more aggressive plant may engulf the other.

Q I received a plant as a gift, and along with it came gnats! Insecticidal soap didn't work. Watering less seems to help, but as soon as I water, the gnats are back. Do you have any pointers?

Peggy Haskin RACINE, WISCONSIN

Melinda: Fungus gnats are those annoying insects that look like small fruit flies flitting around the house. Controlling immature fungus gnats, which are wormlike larvae that feed on organic matter in the soil, eliminates the problem. Fortunately, there is an organic option. *Bacillus thuringiensis israliensis* (Bti) is a naturally occurring bacterium that kills the fungus gnat larvae, mosquitoes and black flies. Mosquito Bits, a Bti product, has been approved for controlling fungus gnats and is available at garden centers, retail outlets and online. Just sprinkle the bits on the soil surface and water. When the fungus gnat larvae feed upon the Bti, they die. Best of all, the product is safe for pets, people and wildlife.

Q This flower was given to me by my 92-year-old neighbor, who has since passed away. It blooms all summer until I put it in the basement to rest over the winter. Can you tell me its name?

Annette Godby KINGS MILLS, OHIO

Melinda: This beauty is sometimes called hot water plant and is botanically known as *Achimenes*. It's a relative of African violet and hardy only in Zones 10 and 11. You clearly know how to care for this summer bloom, but here are a few tips for other interested readers. Grow *Achimenes* in containers filled with African violet potting mix. Keep the soil moist, and fertilize plants regularly throughout the summer growing season. Then bring them indoors before the first fall frost and allow them to rest over winter.

Q What type of dragonfly is this? It frequents our backyard, and we'd never seen a red dragonfly.

Chris Fisher VANCOUVER, WASHINGTON

Kenn and Kimberly: You're right, red is not a common color for dragonflies. This beauty is called a flame skimmer, and you're lucky to have it in your yard. Although flame skimmers are common in some parts of the West, they enter the state of Washington only in your area, just north of the Oregon border. Some smaller types of red dragonflies, called meadowhawks, are more widespread, so you might see those elsewhere in Washington.

Q Do you have any tips for preventing squirrels from digging in my potted plants? I've tried mothballs and repellent sprays, but nothing seems to work.

Mary Rumbaugh MIDLAND, MICHIGAN

Melinda: Squirrels are very persistent and often destructive pests of container plantings. They have grown accustomed to humans and have all day to find ways to overcome barriers. It will take a variety of tactics and persistence on your part to keep them away. Try treating your plants with cayenne pepper as you plant, or use scare tactics, like motion-sensitive sprinklers and pinwheels. Cover new plantings with fine netting to allow air, light and water through but discourage digging. The squirrels may lose interest and move on. Once plants are established, remove the covering and monitor for squirrel damage.

Q On a recent outing to Horicon Marsh in Wisconsin, I captured a photo of this bird among some Canada geese. What kind is it?

Lynette Redner DELAVAN, WISCONSIN

Kenn and Kimberly: Snow geese come in two color morphs: one white with black wingtips, the other blue-gray with a white head, often called "blue goose." At a glance, this looks like the latter. But a couple of things about it seem odd, like the mostly black bill— on an adult snow goose the bill should be mostly pink. Being with Canada geese is also suspicious, because snow geese usually travel in flocks of their own. Size might be the key: If it was a lot smaller than the Canada geese, it was probably an odd snow goose. If it was close to their size, it may have been a hybrid.

Q Grackles come to my backyard feeders in large numbers. These intruders discourage the regulars and eat all the sunflower seeds. Do you have any suggestions?

Lois Vander Waerdt ST. LOUIS, MISSOURI

Kenn and Kimberly: It can be frustrating when large flocks of grackles and other blackbirds wreak havoc on feeders, gobbling up enormous amounts of food and chasing away other birds. Fortunately, in most areas, big flocks of blackbirds are likely to visit only a few times per year. When the blackbird flocks show up, try using tube-style feeders that hang in the middle of a wire cage. Smaller birds can access the feeder, but larger ones, like grackles and starlings, can't get through. This type of feeder will keep out blue jays, too, but you can entice them back when the blackbird flocks have moved on.

Croton

Look for common buckeyes in open habitats, such as fields, gardens and roadsides.

Q I bought a croton several years ago because I liked the different colors in the leaves. Now my plant is doing well, but it generates big green leaves. Why aren't they colorful?

Larry Smith HUDSON, NEW HAMPSHIRE

Melinda: Crotons display the best leaf color when grown outdoors or in a sunny window indoors. All plants contain three pigments—chlorophyll (green), carotinoids (yellow and yellow-oranges) and anthocyanins (red and purple). The carotinoids and anthocyanins mask some or all of the green cholorphyll in plants with colorful leaves. In low light conditions the green chlorophyll pigment becomes more pronounced than the other two pigments. Move your plant to a sunnier window and you should see an improvement in the leaf color.

Q This common buckeye has "common" in its name, but I don't often see them in my area. Are they more widespread in other areas of the U.S.?

Lynn Craska BEACON FALLS, CONNECTICUT

Kenn and Kimberly: The "common" in this butterfly's name serves to distinguish it from other species, like mangrove buckeyes and tropical buckeyes, that live in the American tropics. The common buckeye can be quite numerous in southern states. They move northward in summer, sometimes showing up in strong numbers as far north as New England and the Great Lakes. But most years, they are uncommon in your part of Connecticut.

Q We rarely spot any butterflies in our backyard, but for four days straight, this creature visited our sedum blossoms. Is it a butterfly or a moth?

Sharyn Madison CORTLAND, NEW YORK

Kenn and Kimberly: Your visitor is a painted lady, one of the most remarkable butterflies. It's found all over the world and it migrates, too, but is not as regular in its travels as the most famous migratory butterfly, the monarch. Here in North America, painted ladies are most common in the southwestern states, but in some years they move north and east in huge numbers. One such flight happened in late summer and fall 2017. Thousands were seen in New York, New England and the Midwest. Around Denver, Colorado, the flights of painted ladies were so massive that they were detected by weather radar!

Q I can't seem to find information about growing butterfly bushes in containers. How do they fare, and is it worth trying?

Emily Rumpf CATO, NEW YORK

Melinda: Butterfly bushes, as well as other trees, shrubs and perennials, can be grown in containers. You'll have the greatest chance at winter survival by growing plants that are at least one zone hardier than your region. In cold climates, you will need to provide extra winter protection. Move the plants into an unheated garage, and water any time the soil is thawed and dry. Or cover the roots with wood chips and surround with bagged soil or some other type of insulation. Another option is to sink the pot in a vacant part of your garden that is sheltered.

GET GROWING An Inspired Violet butterfly bush (right) is a seedless noninvasive that attracts bees, butterflies and hummingbirds.

ASK THE EXPERTS **245**

Q Spring migration brings colorful birds to central Indiana. Last year, I put out grape jelly for the orioles, but after two weeks, they were gone. What type of nesting habitat do they prefer?

Dave Douglass ROCHESTER, INDIANA

Kenn and Kimberly: When colorful birds stop to visit during spring migration, we always wish more of them would stick around for summer, but we can work on improving backyard habitats for them. Baltimore orioles like to place their nests in tall, leafy trees, such as cottonwoods, elms, sycamores and maples. If you add one of those trees to your landscape, it will take a few years to mature, so in the meantime, entice orioles to stay longer by putting out fresh oranges sliced in half. Hummingbird feeders (with one part sugar to four parts water) also attract orioles.

GO GRAPE!
Orioles eat most fruit jelly varieties, but the classic standby is grape jelly. As a best practice, offer up jelly that doesn't contain artificial sweeteners, colors or flavors.

Ruby-throated
hummingbirds

Q I once moved these beautiful
wildflowers (above) to a garden
bed where they thrived, but when
I moved, I didn't bring any along
to transplant. What are they?

Dwight Randolph ANTIOCH, TENNESSEE

Melinda: These beauties, commonly called Star
of Bethlehem (*Ornithogalum umbellatum*), are
native to Europe, North Africa and the Middle East.
Once planted, they quickly spread and naturalize.
The spring flowering bulbs are hardy in Zones 4 to
9, grow best in full sun or part shade, and do not
tolerate wet soil in summer. Buy bulbs from your
local garden center to plant in fall.

NOTE: Before you add any transplants to your
garden, check to see whether they're invasive in
your area. The site *www.invasiveplantatlas.org* is a
helpful resource. It's one of the best tools available
for avoiding invasive plants, and it's easy to use.

Q Is it necessary to boil the
sugar-water mixture for
hummingbird feeders? I just
stir until the sugar is dissolved.

Amy Kernes BREA, CALIFORNIA

Kenn and Kimberly: Expert opinions differ on the
importance of boiling the mixture. We always do it
to neutralize some impurities that might be in the
water or sugar. Besides, sugar dissolves more easily
in hot water. But as soon as the feeder is outdoors,
contaminants will get into the water anyway, brought
by hummingbirds, insects or just a breeze. So at best,
boiling the mixture keeps it fresh a little longer. If
your water is good and your time is limited, washing
the feeder thoroughly and often is more important
than boiling the sugar-water mixture.

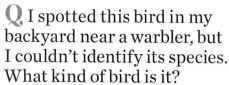

Q I spotted this bird in my backyard near a warbler, but I couldn't identify its species. What kind of bird is it?

Sandra Castle VERO BEACH, FLORIDA

Kenn and Kimberly: This bird is also a warbler, a palm warbler. It spends the summer in spruce forests and bogs in eastern Canada and the northeastern U.S., migrating south to spend winter in southeastern states and around the Caribbean. In Florida, the palm warbler is the second-most commonly seen warbler in winter, after the yellow-rumped warbler. The keys to recognizing it in your photo are the yellow under the tail and the reddish brown cap. Palm warblers often spend time on the ground, hopping about and bobbing their tails up and down.

Q Which type of peanut butter should I feed to birds?

Beth Mucci SWANZEY, NEW HAMPSHIRE

Kenn and Kimberly: Peanut butter is a very good high-protein food for birds, and they eat any of the same types humans do. If you're buying it specifically for birds, look for natural or organic types with the fewest additives. It's best to avoid low-fat varieties, which may not have as much nutritional value for the birds. And if you offer your peanut butter stuffed into holes in a log-type feeder, be sure to clean it out thoroughly before refilling it so mold won't grow on the remains of older contents.

Q I started growing hollyhocks, which bloom for six weeks. How should I care for them once their blooms fade?

Lela Pitts PORUM, OKLAHOMA

Melinda: With their dramatic blooms and ability to attract hummingbirds, hollyhocks are a favorite with gardeners. Hollyhocks are biennials or short-lived perennials. They reseed easily, so continue growing the plants after the blooms fade. This guarantees that the seed will drop. Also, allowing the leaves to grow channels energy to the roots and helps sustain the plant if it is to come back next year. Make sure you wait until the tops turn brown to prune back. Remove the dried stems back to the green rosette of leaves at the base of the plants.

A Carolina wren uses its long bill to reach into a cage feeder for a quick suet treat.

Q **How should I clean my suet cage feeders?**

Chongo Graves APTOS, CALIFORNIA

Kenn and Kimberly: Keeping feeders clean is an important element of bird feeding. Wire cage feeders for serving suet get very messy, so they need regular cleaning, more often in hot weather. Start by soaking the empty feeder in warm water mixed with mild dish detergent and a little vinegar. After it has soaked for an hour or two, wipe off any accumulated gunk with a soft brush or a sponge. Rinse the feeder thoroughly before you refill it and put it back out for the birds.

Milkweed